I0891682

INVISIBLE THREADS

INVISIBLE THREADS

STORIES THAT WEAVE US TOGETHER

STEVEN GARDNER

MADE FOR SUCCESS

Made for Success Publishing
www.MadeForSuccess.com

Copyright © 2026. All rights reserved.

In accordance with the U.S. Copyright Act of 1976, the scanning, uploading, and electronic sharing of any part of this book without the permission of the publisher constitutes unlawful piracy and theft of the author's intellectual property. If you would like to use material from the book (other than for review purposes), prior written permission must be obtained by contacting the publisher at service@madeforsuccess.net. Thank you for your support of the author's rights.

Distributed by Made for Success

First Printing

Library of Congress Cataloging-in-Publication data
Gardner, Steven
Invisible Threads: Stories That Weave Us Together
p. cm.

LCCN: 2025948619
ISBN: 978-1-64146-970-8 *(Hardcover)*
ISBN: 978-1-64146-971-5 *(eBook)*
ISBN: 978-1-64146-972-2 *(Audio)*

Printed in the United States of America

For further information, contact Made for Success Publishing
email service@madeforsuccess.net

For Shell, with love and gratitude.

A Note from the Author

As a writer and photographer, I have taken photographs while writing these stories, which I trust will help visualize the people and personalities featured in the stories.

Please visit Invisible Threads - Steven Gardner at https://www.stevengardnerphotography.com/Invisible-Threads to see the people featured throughout this book.

Dr. Steven Gardner

Contents

MR. KELLETT

As gangly fourteen-year-old boys in a leafy Boston suburb, my teammates and I were psyched to test our mettle on the football field against freshman teams from the small towns west of the city. Perhaps more important than the potential for on-field heroics, however, was the more primal hope of gaining the attention of our cheerleaders. Those *tweeners* on the precarious cusp of womanhood wore grey pleated miniskirts, white sweaters with giant maroon *W*s on the front, and bounced around in ways that seemed to defy gravity.

If a play on the field went improbably well for one of us—occasionally, even yours truly—you might even hear them chanting, "Steve Gardner, he's our man—if he can't do it, no one can!" An ode to joy, if ever there was one for a boy of fourteen.

I was the quarterback of the team, and before our Friday afternoon games, I routinely met with our head coach, Jeremiah Kellett, to go over the plays we would be using that day. (Before those meetings, I sometimes spent time in the boys' room losing my stomach contents, but I made sure nobody knew about that.) Our playbook was not complicated—four or five basic running plays on each side of the center and a similar number of pass plays. And, of course, the quarterback sneak.

When the games started and our team got the ball, Mr. Kellett would signal the plays to me from the sideline. He was an easygoing man, about thirty years old, with a Roman nose, intense dark eyes, and hairy, muscular legs. (In those days, the high school coaches wore football pants for reasons lost to history.)

If Mr. Kellett wanted me to call a sweep, where I pitched the ball to a running back who would try to run around one end of the line, he would extend his arm straight out to the appropriate side. If he wanted me to pass the ball to a particular receiver, he would fan out his fingers above his head and make a motion like tossing a Frisbee to one side of the field. If anybody on the opposing sideline had been watching this with even minimal alertness, it would not have been too hard to decipher our system.

Even so, the strategy served us well. We had an elusive runner named Jack Rizzo, who later played briefly for the New York Giants, and a pugnacious receiver named Dilly Lazzari, who had earned that moniker due to his uncanny resemblance to a puppet on the *Howdy Doody Show* with huge ears. After three games, we were undefeated.

The fourth game of the year was on a blustery October day in a neighboring town, a couple of exits west on the Massachusetts Turnpike. There had been an early frost that year, and not a single blade of grass was alive, leaving the field an unforgiving expanse of semi-frozen mud. As usual, Mr. Kellett and I reviewed the plays before the game and talked about general strategies that would apply to circumstances that were likely to come up, say third down and ten yards to go for a first down. In that example, we would probably pass the ball, rather than call a running play.

My friend and co-captain, David Lock, an undersized offensive lineman who obsessively listened to Thelonius Monk on vinyl records at night, walked out to midfield with me for the coin toss. We won the flip of the coin and chose to receive the kickoff. When the other team's kicker launched the ball through the end zone, the ball was spotted on our twenty-yard line.

When I looked over at Mr. Kellett on our sideline for his signal, his hands were folded across his chest. I didn't remember that gesture. Thinking that I must have missed something in our pre-game session, I called a timeout and jogged over to the sideline, aware that it was highly unusual to waste a precious timeout before the very first play of a football game.

"Sorry, coach, I don't remember that signal."

"It's not a signal."

"I'm sorry?"

"I'm not giving you any more signals."

"Oh . . . you want me to get them from one of the assistant coaches?"

"Nope."

"I'm not sure I understand."

"You are going to call the plays yourself from now on."

"Really? But I. . . ."

"I am completely confident that you can handle it. Now go do it."

He turned and walked away.

I jogged out to the huddle and called the first play—one that I was pretty sure Mr. Kellett would have chosen. My head was spinning, and I didn't feel particularly confident, but, for some reason, I acted as if I was. We ended up winning that game and the next three for an undefeated season.

The cheerleaders arranged a celebratory party to honor us, their pubescent heroes, in the linoleum-floored basement of an offensive lineman named Guy Gledhill. A few "popular" couples swayed slowly to love songs by Roy

Orbison and Ricky Nelson, while the "less popular" kids sat self-consciously on folding chairs. We all shared the pleasurable sense that we had just contributed our bit to town pride. The celebration ended when our parents picked us up in station wagons with faux wood panels around midnight. On the ride home, in the back seats of those vehicles, ardent hopes of canoodling with the cheerleaders were met with modest success in a few cases, but abject rejection in others.

Mr. Kellett was a math teacher, but I never had the chance to be in his classroom. The next year, I went away to a prestigious boarding school and essentially never played quarterback again. There were boys there who threw the ball further and ran faster. And the coaches called all the plays.

There was a little loudspeaker mounted at a crooked angle high on the wall of the emergency room at the Boston teaching hospital, where I was a resident doctor. It was early July, and I was just beginning my first rotation in emergency medicine. Every few minutes, the speaker communicated staticky alerts from ambulance crews, notifying the emergency room staff of their ETAs. When the medics feverishly burst through the swinging doors, they would divest themselves of a shocking medley of human beings in improbable forms of distress. Occasionally, the outcomes were amusing, like the time an unfortunate fellow was wheeled in, apparently covered from head to toe in blood. It turned out that the "blood" was actually barn paint that some delinquents had poured on him when they found him sleeping in an alley. Unfortunately, however, most of the souls rushed in on the ambulance stretchers with the strange-looking collapsible legs were perilously close to crossing a fine line into the next world.

On a balmy night a week after I started my residency, I heard an agitated voice with a heavy Boston accent crackle out of the speaker and announce, "This is Boston EMS. We are inbound on Cambridge Street with a thirty-nine-year-old male who was hit by a train and is in full cardiopulmonary arrest. We should be there in two minutes."

For the better part of two hundred years, there had been a terrifying rite of passage at that Boston teaching hospital. At an unannounced time during their first rotation in the emergency room, each of the dozen newly minted "medical house officers" would be abruptly assigned to lead a highly-skilled team of emergency room nurses and doctors in an actual "code blue"—the very real attempt to resuscitate a patient in full arrest. A senior physician with overall responsibility for the ER that day would simply tap one of the rookies on the shoulder without warning and assign them that unnerving responsibility.

Knowing that such a moment was coming was terrifying, and we knew that no amount of practice on a plastic dummy called "Resuscitation Annie" could ever prepare us for a responsibility like that. There were scores of reasons a patient might appear at a city emergency room unconscious or near death. Was it an overdose? Had they choked? Was there fluid around the heart, preventing it from pumping? Was there a stab wound somewhere? The possibilities seemed almost infinite, and the emergency approach to managing each one was different.

In a code blue, decisions must be made in seconds, often with little or no history to go on. It's unrealistic, but the leader of the team is expected to make an accurate initial assessment of the patient's problem and immediately give decisive, potentially life-saving orders or, at least, not make things worse. For a newly minted physician, it was quite impossible to imagine a more intimidating scenario.

An imposing senior physician in a starched Oxford shirt and a bow tie was in charge that summer night. When the loudspeaker crackled, he pointed a bony index finger at me with the severe bearing of a military officer giving orders to a private and said simply, "Gardner, this one is yours."

When a patient in cardiac distress is rushed into the cramped and stunningly bright room reserved for patients who have "crashed"—or are about to—the team leader is tasked with immediately assigning specific roles to the nurses and doctors who materialize magically around the narrow code table. After hearing the operator's Code Blue announcement on the hospital's overhead intercom, any doctors and nurses in the vicinity come running and offer to assist.

In a typical scenario, someone is assigned to perform chest compressions while another person is instructed to draw blood. One person attempts the challenging task of inserting an endotracheal tube to breathe for the patient while another accepts the critically important job of starting an IV. Someone checks the patient's oxygen level in an artery and adjusts oxygen pumping from a cannula into the patient's lungs. A nurse cuts the clothes off the patient with a pair of giant scissors so that someone else can place EKG leads on the chest, arm, and leg, making it possible to see the patient's heart rhythm on an overhead monitor. Another nurse tries to access the patient's bladder to see if the kidneys have shut down and stopped producing urine by inserting a catheter through the penis or by prying open a woman's vulva in the midst of total chaos. Needles, test tubes, and splatters of blood fly everywhere, while a technician appears from the laboratory with a liter bag of O-negative blood, the type that can be transfused to any patient from a "universal donor." A senior nurse works a nearby phone, frantically trying to get information about the patient from family members, if she can locate any.

When done with impeccable professionalism, this frenetic and seemingly disjointed collection of actions can be completed in less than a minute. Then, in the pregnant moments that follow, all eyes turn to the team leader who is presumed to have figured out, at least generally, what's going on. While scanning the EKG tracing on the monitor, that person is expected to bark out precise orders to the assembled group that will keep a fellow human being among the living.

The right leg of the nameless man being rushed in on the stretcher that night was mangled and appeared to be connected to his torso by only a tenuous flap of skin. He was ghostly white. Blood trickled from his mouth and, more alarmingly, spurted from a massive gash halfway down the right side of his rib cage. He had an unkempt beard, smelled badly, and appeared to be a homeless man familiar to some of the staff, a so-called "frequent flyer."

Anticipating this rite of passage was so unnerving that everyone in our residency class had carefully studied what to do in the most common cardiac arrest scenarios. For example, if the patient was experiencing an abnormal heart rhythm called *ventricular fibrillation*, we all knew that the immediate response was to shock the heart with paddles and administer anti-arrhythmic medicines through an IV catheter. We carefully memorized the doses of those drugs for "V-fib" and the order in which they should be given.

The problem was the innumerable other scenarios that might bring somebody into the ER in critical condition. We memorized the actions that needed to be taken immediately in the most common ones, but how valuable would that memorization be, we wondered, in the perilous moments after we were assigned the responsibility of resuscitating a fellow human being who was knocking on Heaven's door?

Once my patient was hooked up to the monitor, I studied the screen above the gurney. There was no electrical activity at all. This was *asystole* (a-cis-toe-lee) or "flatline," meaning the patient's heart was not working at all. Whether due to massive blood loss or extensive damage to the heart muscle itself, his heart had completely stopped.

Like all of my overachieving residency colleagues, I had memorized the algorithm that needed to be followed in the flatline scenario, and a faint sense of relief passed through me. I ordered epinephrine and atropine to be given immediately through the IV tube in an effort to stimulate the heart and a bolus of an even more powerful drug that is injected in an effort to reverse shock. When there was no response to those medicines, we made a last-resort effort to get the heart beating by inserting a pacemaker wire directly through the rib cage into the patient's heart. Unsurprisingly, that effort was unsuccessful, as it invariably is at that stage of an arrest.

Seven or eight minutes elapsed while medical students pumped feverishly on the patient's chest and blood samples were sent to the lab with technicians who literally ran off with them down the corridor.

The man's oxygen level was critically low now, and a massive amount of carbon dioxide had built up in his body, a combination that is inconsistent with life. Despite multiple transfusions and a medication to correct a severe acid-base imbalance in his blood, nothing we did worked. The pacemaker was not capturing the heart, and no meaningful cardiac function had resulted from our efforts. The patient was blue and lifeless, and everyone on the team knew that any faint hope that his brain could survive that long without oxygen was essentially gone.

I shone a flashlight into the man's eyes. The pupils were dilated and did not react whatsoever to the light. The EKG monitor revealed the same continuous flat line that we had watched since his arrival. I asked the gifted nurses and doctors around the table if anyone had any additional ideas.

When they shook their heads, I looked up at the big wall clock behind the patient and heard myself say, "We can stop. Time of death: 2:41 AM. Thank you, everybody."

Years later, looking back on my career, I was aware that I had benefited from the teachings of many remarkable people in various schools and in the hospitals where I learned medicine. Some had forced me to memorize arcane things like Avogadro's number (6.02×10^{23}) and something inscrutable called the Krebs Cycle. Others had passed on more important human lessons, like how to assist someone who is very sick and does not speak your language. Those latter lessons I learned from scintillating mentors like Dr. Kate Treadway and Dr. John Stoeckle at Massachusetts General Hospital.

But when I thought about what Coach Jeremiah Kellett revealed to me on the sidelines of a frozen football field at age fourteen, I wondered if that might have been the single most important lesson anyone had ever taught me.

A high school classmate told me that Mr. Kellett had retired and lived year-round on Cape Cod. By report, he was an active senior who played tennis and golf practically every day during the summer and was an avid fisherman. He lived in South Dennis, only six miles across the ocean from Martha's Vineyard, where my son, Graham, and I were ensconced at Camp Jabberwocky, the iconic sleepover camp for kids and adults with disabilities, where I was a volunteer doctor. I found Mr. Kellett's phone number, and on a halcyon day in late June, he accepted my invitation to come over to the island for a visit.

He was in his early eighties by then, but looked much younger when he strode confidently off the ferry at Oak Bluffs. He still had the wiry build of an athlete and had not put on a paunch. He had a good head of hair with only touches of grey under a Red Sox cap.

I introduced Jerry—it felt strange to call him by his first name—to the zany world of Camp Jabberwocky, where we spent the day. He immediately sensed what was going on there in the woods of Vineyard Haven, where a collection of individuals with and without disabilities was noisily sharing the joys of summer on that scenic island. And it was great fun for me to introduce my old coach to my beautiful son, who, like many of the campers, had cerebral palsy.

When the campers gathered for dinner, I drove Mr. Kellett back to the ferry terminal for the short ride to the mainland. We had budgeted a little extra time to visit at the famous Black Dog Cafe before the boat left, and we sat down at a booth with a spectacular view of the harbor.

The time had come for me to thank him for the lesson he had given me so many years earlier, the one that had served me so well in my medical training and throughout my life. I started by telling him about how I had nervously survived the rite of passage as a resident doctor in the emergency room, attempting to resuscitate the man who had been hit by a train. As I was relating that story to him, it occurred to me for the first time that the number of people around the table in that crash room was possibly the exact number of people in the offensive huddle of a football team.

I told him that his challenge to "call the plays yourself" had prepared me for many situations in my life where decisions had to be made despite having imperfect information to base them on. Decisions I didn't feel comfortable making. Decisions about a child with a disability. Decisions about family and relationships. Decisions about patients who were counting on me to assist them during vulnerable times in their lives. It was a poignant thing, thanking a teacher that way after so many years. When I looked Mr. Kellett in the eye, I felt my emotions rising.

We didn't speak for a few seconds, but our eyes communicated and moistened a little. For a moment, I felt as if we had just agreed upon a game strategy and were about to head out to the football field. Jerry—it was still hard for me to call him that—thanked me for the opportunity to visit Camp Jabberwocky and for reaching out to him.

A man announced that the ferry was ready to board, and we stood up, feeling a little awkward. We walked the short distance to the dock in silence and shook hands.

"I am proud of you and Graham," said Mr. Kellett with a broad smile, before turning and walking up the gangway without looking back.

After Graham passed away and I wrote the book, *Jabberwocky: Lessons of Love from a Boy Who Never Spoke*, I mailed Mr. Kellett a copy with a note. Having visited

Camp Jabberwocky and met Graham, I was pretty sure that the story would resonate with him. About a month later, I received this handwritten note from my old coach in my mailbox at home:

> *Doctor Steve,*
>
> *I read every word of Jabberwocky—some of them many times. Each night I watched the news and then went to your book. Thus, I went from the world of despair and destruction to Graham's world of kind people, hope and love.*
>
> *It is truly a love story and beautifully written. Thank you for sharing.*
>
> *Jerry Kellett*

JABBERWOCKY

Jabberwocky, The Poem:

"And hast thou slain the Jabberwock?
Come to my arms, my beamish boy!
O frabjous day! Callooh! Callay!
He chortled in his joy."
—Through the Looking Glass by Lewis Carroll

Jabberwocky, The Camp:

"On an island off the southern coast of Massachusetts, there is a place where hope flourishes. The island is Martha's Vineyard. The place is Camp Jabberwocky, a small summer camp for the disabled situated in the woods not too far from Lake Tashmoo. Jabberwocky emerged in the early 1950s. It began in a time when public sentiment regarding the role of disabled people in society was dismal. Services were minimal and rights were not yet an issue. Nonetheless, Jabberwocky sprang forth. The camp started as

a small experiment: a handful of children, a tiny summer cottage, a director and a young assistant. From there camp has grown to a fourteen-acre site, seventeen buildings and a large volunteer staff. It now serves about one hundred children and adults every summer. But this is only the beginning . . . ."

—A Brief History of the Martha's Vineyard Cerebral Palsy Camp

I watched in awe as Pete Halby picked Graham up out of his wheelchair and threw him high into the afternoon sky. Beyond them, golden sunlight glistened on dozens of triangular sails, far out on the cobalt blue waters of Nantucket Sound.

It was the first summer that my handsome nine-year-old son and I were spending together at Camp Jabberwocky, and I was beginning to realize that we had joined a kind of parallel universe, one that existed just six miles across the ocean from the world we left behind when we boarded the big ferry in Woods Hole earlier that same day.

When we arrived on the island of Martha's Vineyard that dazzling summer afternoon, Graham as a camper and I as a first-time camp physician, I immediately noticed a hand-painted phrase on the back door of one of the Camp minivans that greeted us at the dock in Vineyard Haven: "The best way to explain it is to do it."

I wondered about that expression at the time and, even after twenty-five years as a volunteer doctor at Camp Jabberwocky, I am just now beginning to understand what it means.

Jabberwocky is not easy to describe. It's a kind of haven where people with all kinds of abilities and disabilities come together for several weeks in a picture-postcard setting to share the fun of summer, test limits, and experience life vividly. During their time on the island, the campers and counselors live in the present. Playfulness and whimsicality are celebrated. Outrageousness is encouraged. By summer's end, compassion, laughter, and love have turned an eclectic collection of individuals into a rambunctious extended family.

I knew little of Camp Jabberwocky, however, on that first day of the thirteen summer sessions I would ultimately spend there with my son, who was unable to speak or stand on his own due to cerebral palsy. There wasn't much time for us to get oriented because, immediately after arriving "on island," our tumultuous entourage boarded Camp's signature red bus and assorted minivans and headed straight to the shore for a cookout.

At State Beach, the magnificent sandy expanse on the northeast side of the island, the percussionist Rick Bausman and his spirited drum ensemble were set up in the sand, playing Haitian-based rhythms. The sun was descending in the glowing sky to the west, giving a golden hue to the clear afternoon light. The warm air was pungent as the smell of the sea mingled with the first barbecue scents of the season.

Bursting with anticipation, Jabberwocky's campers were pushed and, in some cases, carried down to the beach where dancing erupted instantly. The campers who could stand did so and whirled around wildly with their counselors. Others danced with abandon while seated in their wheelchairs. Everyone was ready to *boogie.* In those moments, I began to understand that letting go of inhibition is an integral part of the Jabberwocky experience.

Pete Halby, an exuberant counselor and non-stop instigator of fun and mischief, had spent summers on the island throughout his life. I watched as he asked Graham if he wanted to join the dance. Although Graham was nonverbal, his eyes showed that he was up for it. My own eyes widened as Pete unbuckled Graham, picked him up out of his wheelchair, and threw him in the air!

For the next hour, Pete carried Graham in his arms, intermittently tossing him up like a giant bean bag. They merrily bopped around the circle of drummers, weaving in and out among the other revelers.

Wendy Grey, then a medical student, was carrying Scott Scherer, a youngster with cerebral palsy who was beaming from ear to ear, and I watched with fascination as the pair danced with abandon at the edge of the gentle surf. In that golden hour before sunset, everyone in the Jabberwocky family seemed to be cavorting without the slightest self-consciousness.

I looked over at Graham bouncing crazily in Pete's arms. He returned my gaze with a giant grin on his face, as if to say, "Dad, the best way to explain it is to do it!"

A few weeks later, on a warm summer evening just after sunset, I was feeling slightly grumpy.

I had been at Camp all day, dealing with a string of generally minor medical issues. I was tired from the frenetic activity of Jabberwocky and the intense emotions that I always feel there. While those feelings are powerfully positive, they can be draining sometimes.

Just as I was about to go back to what was then referred to as the "Doctor's House," a small home that Camp Jabberwocky owns just down the street, one of the counselors asked me to check on a camper in Bandersnatch. (The cabins are named after characters from the famous Lewis Carroll poem about the Jabberwock.) She was concerned about an impish youngster named Jonah who had CP and depended on others for all his daily needs.

Jonah had severe spasticity and was in the habit of sleeping on his belly, insisting with grimaces that it was the only way that he could get comfortable in bed. As a result, though, he had developed painful friction sores on the front of his lower thighs and kneecaps.

I trudged up to see him in the twilight of that perfect June evening. Cicadas were buzzing. There was a gentle breeze in the scrub oaks that shelter the campus. I could faintly hear the lyrical pinging of a bell buoy out in Vineyard Haven harbor. Lights were on in the cabins around Camp, and muted chatter, laughter, and singing mingled pleasantly in the quiet air around Bandersnatch.

After seeing Jonah's abrasions, I decided to apply antibiotic ointment to the scraped areas and dress them with a non-stick bandage, anticipating that we would need to repeat that procedure for the next few nights. I went back out to gather the supplies from our modest clinic in the main cabin.

As I walked, I wondered what I was doing. It was a glorious summer evening on one of the most beautiful islands in the world. I imagined that, at that very moment, some of my old school pals might be sitting on the deck of a graceful sailboat in Edgartown Harbor, sipping gin and tonics and looking up at the stars with not a care in the world. I envisioned well-heeled vacationers laughing by candlelight over lobster dinners in elegant night spots around the island.

By contrast, I was dirty and exhausted, about to return to a stuffy cabin on a trivial first aid mission for a disabled kid from Indiana whom I had never even heard speak. And, like almost everyone at camp, I was a volunteer. If I were going to take care of people during my precious vacation time, wouldn't it be smarter to do something that involved getting paid?

In that grouchy state of mind, I opened the creaky screen door to Bandersnatch and sat on the edge of Jonah's wooden bunk. The faint scent of Coppertone and wet towels hung in the still air of the cabin. A big laundry basket in the middle of the room overflowed with T-shirts, socks, and bathing suits. In the semidarkness, it didn't take long to apply the ointment and dressings and turn Jonah back on his belly. I said a cursory "Good night" and pushed open the screen door to leave. But just as the door closed, I thought I heard a sound coming from Jonah's bunk. I went back in.

"Jonah, did you say something?"

Indeed, in a faint, halting voice delivered with great effort, I heard him speak for the first time.

"Ankyoo Dahdhastee."

"What's that, Jonah, I didn't quite hear you?"

"Ankyoo Dahdastee."

"Jonah, I'm sorry. I'm not understanding you. Try one more time."

On his third try, I finally got it. In what turned out to be one of my life's most wondrous epiphanies, I clearly heard Jonah say, "Thank you, Doctor Steve."

In the poignant moments that followed, I felt the full pathos of Jonah's condition. There was no denying that his circumstances were challenging. But we were together at Camp Jabberwocky, where it is difficult to be gloomy for long. I sat for a few moments, marveling at the grace of the little boy lying patiently on his belly in the twilight, and rubbed the back of his head.

"You're very welcome, Jonah. We'll do the same thing tomorrow night. I hope you have a good sleep."

When I pushed open the creaky screen door of Bandersnatch for the final time that evening and emerged into that splendid summer night, I was not jealous of anyone in the world.

I knew that I was exactly where I was meant to be.

Later that summer, the pioneering organization called AccesSportAmerica, led by its irrepressible founder, the Reverend Ross Lily, brought high challenge water sports to Camp Jabberwocky. The setting was a sparkling three-mile-long body of shallow water on the northeast side of the island, just inside the barrier beach that faces Nantucket Sound. Close to the road, free of big waves and dotted with sand bars and salt marshes, the coastal lagoon was the perfect setting to introduce exhilarating water sports to the campers of Jabberwocky. Sengekontacket (Singe-a-con-tack-it) is the lyrical name the Native Americans gave to that place of transcendent beauty.

For a few days, hoping to make even a small contribution to this new Jabberwocky adventure, I minimally helped the AccesSport team on the water and on the beach. I was, by no means, an accomplished windsurfer, but I was experienced enough to stay out of the water—most of the time. Along with the Jabberwocky counselors, I helped load campers on and off windsurfers, kayaks, and inner tubes.

Then, on a magnificent day in early July with a light onshore breeze, Ross asked if I wanted to take Graham out on the special windsurfer he had invented for his son, Josh, who had CP. The rig had a plastic chair secured to the board.

My heart soared!

Ross strapped Graham into the seat after we donned life vests, and he pushed us off into Sengekontacket. The wind was light, and the special board was stable. The calm water sparkled around us. As I stood, straddling Graham's chair, arms wrapped around him, we tacked eastward toward Edgartown before coming about and riding the downwind leg back toward the gentle cliffs of Farm Neck. As we glided through the tranquil water that morning, Graham was able to briefly place his hands over mine on the "boom" and experience the feeling of controlling our sail.

My son and I shared something sublime in those moments. The exquisite beauty of the setting, the warmth of the sun, and the thrill of moving together over the water, powered only by the wind, combined to make it an indelible, transformative experience.

On the lagoon that morning, Graham and I discovered a breathtaking sense of freedom. We were proud to have participated in a challenging sport, and we sensed that we had moved in harmony with a stunning sliver of the natural world. For both of us, it would be the most thrilling athletic experience of a lifetime.

Thanks to that early inspiration from AccesSportAmerica, Graham and I later learned to ski, kayak, and cycle together on modified equipment. Each of those sports was wonderful for us in its own way.

But nothing would ever compare to that shimmering morning on Sengekontacket when we rode the wind together on Ross and Josh's windsurfer.

Before we headed home that first summer, a very special celebration took place at Camp. And we were *all* invited. The entire eclectic Jabberwocky family with its kaleidoscopic spectrum of abilities and disabilities. The whole madcap collection of individuals from wildly different backgrounds—*all of us.* The pleasure of our company was requested! We were cordially invited! To our wonder and delight, Camp Jabberwocky was about to participate in that most joyous of summer celebrations: a wedding!

This marriage ceremony would be particularly poignant because Jonathan Wolf and Mandy Adams were two of our own. Destined for careers in teaching and advocacy for the homeless, the couple had met at Camp as counselors several years earlier and fallen in love. Their families loved the Vineyard and were longtime Jabberwocky supporters. On an island known for gala events, this wedding promised to be the most romantic and magnificent social happening of the summer. Side by side with some well-heeled summer residents and visitors, we were all going to be part of it. Indeed, the wedding party itself, the bridesmaids and groomsmen, was to feature a sprinkling of campers and counselors.

Naturally, there are elegant venues on Martha's Vineyard available for prominent social occasions, including yacht clubs and country clubs. But Jonathan and Mandy wanted their ceremony to be held on Camp Jabberwocky's campus. A big tent appeared in the field at the back of the property, decorated with huge yellow and blue ribbons and vibrant bouquets of the island's signature flowers, blue hydrangeas. Anticipation was intense as the special day approached.

On the morning of the wedding, the Jabberwocky counselors, exuberant young people of imagination and kindness, scrubbed and coiffed their campers until they literally sparkled. Elegant finery from the "costume cabin" in the basement of Camp's theater replaced funky shorts and T-shirts. Two by two, the pairs of counselors and campers arrived for the ceremony, many approaching the tent in walkers and wheelchairs.

Under a dappled canopy of scrub oaks, I walked behind my son's wheelchair as he was pushed along by his counselor. A musician was seated near an improvised altar playing the guitar and quietly singing "It's a Wonderful World." My heart was full as I reflected on the bride and groom's choice to be married at Jabberwocky, a place defined by mutual support and love.

As the wedding congregation proceeded along the path to the big field, steeped in the sense of quiet reverence that surrounds a wedding, we witnessed a perfectly timed example of Camp Jabberwocky's playful *irreverence.* Someone had posted a handcrafted message on a tree for Mandy and Jonathan to see: "Turn back now!"

At the ceremony, Graham was at one end of an arc of wheelchairs to the right of the wedding party. I sat in the grass next to him, rested my arm on his, and experienced the service at his side. I could not remember feeling the way I did in those moments ever before in my life.

And yet, it would not have been Camp Jabberwocky if the service had not been punctuated by laughter. A whimsical interlude was provided by our Camp directors that year, JoJo and Arthur, when they stood up and recited the Jabberwocky poem with zest and theatricality:

> *"The Jabberwocky with eyes of flame*
> *Came whiffling through the tulgey wood*
> *And burbled as it came!"*

Moments later, under a beautiful chuppah, the symbolic tapestry that forms a protective wedding "canopy" over the bride and groom, Rabbi Rachel Cowan spoke to Mandy and Jonathan about Camp Jabberwocky:

"Here you are surrounded and blessed by God's presence, open to everyone coming into your life. Chance, randomness, and destiny have come together in this moment. This is where your love grows deep. This is where you feel deeply at home. This is where you overcome fears, take risks, and grow. This is where you need a tremendous sense of humor! This is where you give and receive support. This is where you can be exactly who you are. This is where you trust your instincts and know you make a difference. This is where your hearts have no walls."

In the exquisite moments that followed, family, friends, campers, and volunteers bore witness as the couple exchanged wedding vows. On the most important day of their lives, Mandy and Jonathan chose to include all of Camp Jabberwocky. They wanted us to know that the God blessing their marriage loves all of us, unconditionally.

MARATHON MONDAY

I set my alarm early on the third Monday in April, known in New England as "Marathon Monday," and drove out to the sleepy town of Hopkinton, Massachusetts. After parking my car, I wandered around with my camera among some thirty thousand runners and wheelchair athletes in the emotionally charged minutes before they would start their grueling journey to Boston. By the way, when you *drive* to Hopkinton from Boston in a Jeep Grand Cherokee going seventy miles per hour on the Massachusetts Turnpike, 26.2 miles seems like a long way. And it is. Unless you grow up in the high plains of Kenya, your body is not really designed to run that far.

In the morning chill, I meandered through a big field near the town green where runners waited in groups for their starting times to be announced. Men and women lost in unfathomable thought lay on their backs on old tarps and blankets that they would abandon there, gazing up into an ashen sky. Others sat quietly with their eyes closed, listening to music through headphones. A few moved around restlessly, even jogging in place. I noticed that many of those people had photographs pinned to their running shorts or sleeveless T-shirts known as *singlets.*

There was a palpable sense of expectation on that field, a collective awareness that a once-in-a-lifetime experience was about to reveal itself. Those people were about to attempt something extremely difficult—maybe even the single hardest thing that they had ever set out to do. But, beyond the awareness of the daunting physical challenge that lay ahead, I saw something more poignant on the faces of many of those runners, and I was pretty sure it had to do with the photos clipped to their shirts and shorts.

The snapshots revealed the faces of people who appeared to be facing adversity of some kind. In many cases, a diagnosis of cancer was a good bet. Some of the images were of people who faced adversity with grace and dignity, but were possibly no longer here. Either way, it was apparent that, for many of those everyday people biding time on that field in Hopkinton, the punishing experience they were about to undertake was nothing less than a profound expression of support and love for someone else.

The vast majority of the five hundred thousand spectators waiting for them on the road to Boston seemed to understand how that sort of motivation could prompt someone to attempt a thing as crazy as running more than twenty-six miles on a cold, dreary day. And on the roads and sidewalks of seven towns and cities, including a quarter-mile stretch of manic cheering at Wellesley College called the *scream tunnel,* those spectators were poised to fanatically shout out their support.

On that drab morning, it was clear that—for the runners and spectators alike—the Boston Marathon was more than an insanely long road race. For many of those who set out from Hopkinton, it is a kind of metaphor in which the running itself is a physical symbol of something more abstract. What is *more abstrac*t is the profound love those runners feel for another human being. Someone who, quite possibly, is about to attempt an even more challenging journey at a cancer center in Boston or elsewhere.

On the village green in Hopkinton, the collective emotion of thirty thousand human beings was like an electric current you could literally feel in the air. In moments, cheered on by half a million souls who *understood,* their journey was about to begin. From that field of brown grass that had not yet come back to life in the chill of the early New England springtime, ordinary people were about to merge onto a winding road of shared humanity that would carry them up—and beyond—a place called Heartbreak Hill.

On a crisp April morning a decade later, I positioned my ten-year-old son's wheelchair on the sidewalk in Wellesley Hills, about halfway between Hopkinton and Boston. There was electricity in the air as playful students from Wellesley College loaded cups of Gatorade and plates of orange wedges onto folding tables at the midpoint of the marathon. A few yellow daffodils and purple crocuses poked through lingering patches of dirty snow in flower beds behind us, a welcome coda to an interminable New England winter.

Like the five hundred thousand other souls sick of being trapped indoors, we had ventured out into the still-chilly air that day to celebrate the country's oldest road race, which—in our part of the world—is the quintessential harbinger of springtime.

Anticipation grew as we waited for the lead pack of runners to materialize over a small hill to our west. Graham and I had watched from that same spot the year before, and we knew that, in a minute or two, elite athletes from Kenya, Ethiopia, Japan, and maybe even an American or two, would fly past us on feet that seemed to barely touch the pavement. Accompanying them would be an uninterrupted roar of passionate encouragement that would propel them up the hills in Newton and on to the finish line in Copley Square.

News helicopters hovered above the lead pack that was still just out of our sight, and the cheering swelled like an approaching windstorm. Suddenly, there they were—a dozen wafer-thin men in neon-colored shoes running astonishingly fast without apparent effort. And equally suddenly, they were gone, disappearing eastward in a tight pack. A few minutes later, thousands of weekend warriors with pained expressions began to sweep past us in ever-growing throngs, many of them with snapshots clipped to their singlets and shorts.

Some ten minutes after the lead runners flew by, there was an audible commotion beyond the little hill. It was cheering, but this time with a different pitch and intensity. The sound swelled as it approached us from the west until it had the urgency of an approaching tornado, a roar that was louder than the reaction to a walk-off home run at Fenway Park. And it was building.

Emerging over the rise in the road, we saw what appeared to be a stocky middle-aged man pushing something. Moments later, we realized that the *something* he was pushing was a slender man seated in a racing wheelchair. We recognized then that the middle-aged man was Dick Hoyt and the person he was pushing was his son, Rick, who had spastic cerebral palsy. Over the years, the pair had become New England icons, eventually completing an astonishing thirty-two Boston Marathons together and becoming a beloved "institution within an institution," as the *Boston Globe* put it.

There was no way not to get goosebumps while witnessing the spectators' impassioned reaction to the Hoyts. The love and grit embodied by Rick and Dick stirred powerful emotions in the huge crowd. In those moments, the differences and divisions among all those witnesses seemed to blur or even disappear altogether.

Ten years after the unthinkable terror attacks on the Boston Marathon in 2013, the typically overflowing emotions at the finish line near the Boston Public Library were even more intense than usual. I watched from temporary bleachers along Boylston Street with friends from the Spaulding Rehabilitation Hospital, the incredible facility that cared for so many of the victims after that unspeakable tragedy.

Now, on a warm, sun-splashed April day, the singularly festive atmosphere of Marathon Monday was palpable again at the finish line and throughout the city.

Some of the approaching runners had entered the race in 2013, only to be turned back just short of the finish when the bombs went off. A few were so close to the explosions that they lost their hearing, and their clothes were smoking as they stumbled away from Copley Square. Completing the marathon a decade later was their way of raising a middle finger to people filled with hate.

Only about twenty yards from where the bombs had exploded, we watched a group of Marines improbably cross the finish line in camouflage uniforms and combat boots, running to honor the memory of a brother who was killed in action in Afghanistan.

We watched Cameron Hoyt, the grandson and nephew of Dick and Rick, who was running the Boston Marathon for "Team Hoyt" to continue the family's legacy of "*Yes You Can*," following the deaths of his grandfather and uncle.

We watched a man with Parkinson's disease painfully shuffle across the finish line, followed closely by a young man with Down syndrome who collapsed into the collective embrace of his family.

We watched blind runners, tethered by strings to their "guides," finishing with arms raised in triumph.

We saw people complete the race on one, and even two, prosthetic legs.

We watched a stunning number of wheelchair athletes practically fly across the finish line, which was painted in the marathon's iconic blue and yellow colors.

We watched big groups of nurses and doctors running in teams representing the great Boston teaching hospitals, those astonishing places where "any person in distress becomes our neighbor."

We saw clusters of distinctly non-elite athletes wobble across the line hand in hand, many with small photos clipped to their clothes, raising awareness for scores of issues, including suicide prevention and autism research.

Comic relief has historically been a feature of the marathon, and 2023 was no exception. Interspersed among the many poignant scenes at the finish line were a man dressed as a rhinoceros, several versions of Elvis, a giant testicle (to promote awareness of testicular cancer), a gaggle of gnomes, SpongeBob, Forrest Gump, and four hairy guys in Speedos.

Technically, running is easier when there are people ahead of you blocking a headwind. In cycling and distance running, it's called *drafting*. Metaphorically, the hundreds of thousands of elite athletes and ordinary people who have covered the 26.2 miles from Hopkinton to Boston since the first race in 1897 have broken the wind for the runners of today. People like Rick and Dick Hoyt have shown us that it is *possible* to achieve something that initially seems close to *impossible.* And when ordinary people strive to accomplish something this difficult—in honor of another person—something indefinable begins to happen. Something that elevates not just that other person, but perhaps even an entire community.

On the third Monday each April, Boston becomes a metaphor for the entire world. People from many places struggle together over the same twenty-six unforgiving miles, carrying similar dreams. They want to run with other people in a peaceful world. They want to feel safe. They want to challenge themselves and have fun testing their limits. They want to passionately support the people they love through life's joys and, especially, its challenges.

Over arduous months, some thirty thousand runners and wheelchair athletes lace up sneakers and train for this incredible test for highly personal reasons. But on Marathon Monday, they run together as a kind of eclectic family, carrying with them the passionate hope that none of us will ever have to face adversity alone.

A STARFISH STORY

A young girl was walking along a beach upon which thousands of starfish had been washed up during a terrible storm. When she came to each starfish, she would pick it up and throw it back into the ocean.

She had been doing this for some time when an old man approached her and said, "Little girl, why are you doing this? Look at this beach! You can't save all these starfish."

The girl initially seemed crushed. But after a few moments, she bent down, picked up another starfish, and hurled it as far as she could into the ocean. Then she looked up at the man and replied, "I saved that one."

—Adapted from Loren C. Eiseley's The Star Thrower

Zhou Lin ("Joline") was ten years old at the time of the explosion that left her hands, abdomen, and feet in flames, irrevocably changing her life. The heat from the ensuing fire was so intense that the fabric from her clothing was burned into her skin. Her younger sister, five-year-old Zhou Jing, had burns on her face but suffered less extensive injuries than Joline.

The accident occurred in 2003 in a remote farming village in the province of Sichuan in western China. Before the fire, Guo Chunmei, the girls' mother, and Zhou Zhiping, their father, would rise at dawn, wake their daughters, and prepare porridge with pickled vegetables for breakfast, adding hard-boiled eggs, noodles, and rice balls on special days. After feeding their pigs and chickens, all four would walk to nearby fields and work until dark, picking string beans, corn, eggplant, and sweet potatoes. The punishing work was done entirely by hand. Little Zhou Jing was like a "tail," following Joline everywhere. On their lunch break, the family sat in the shade and ate rice with occasional stir-fry dishes, soups, noodles, or dumplings.

All the land in China was technically the property of the communist government, with small parcels allotted to families like Joline's to "own" for growing vegetables or to "sell" to other families. The Chinese *patrilineal* system, which had been in place for centuries, relegated Joline and her sister to secondary roles in the family and in the community. Even within her own extended family, Joline's grandmothers regarded her with contempt and sometimes mocked her for no apparent reason. Thankfully, the archaic practice of "foot binding" young girls had been condemned, but female infanticide and selective abortions of female embryos were lingering legacies of the discrimination against girls. Attendance at local schools was dependent on whether a family had money, with preference given to boys, but at age eight or nine, Joline managed to attend a few classes at the local school in science and English. Most of her time, though, was spent planting, tending, and harvesting crops with Guo Chunmei and Zhou Zhiping.

At the time of the accident, the family lived in a house called a *keekwilee*, a small hut-like structure made from clay and bricks, with an outdoor privy. It was a multigenerational home, with Joline's grandparents sharing the limited space. The supply of electricity was erratic in their remote Sichuan district and, frequently, the family used candles to light the main room in the evening. On the kitchen table of Joline's *keekwilee*, there was a single oil lamp that was used at times to supplement the candlelight. Zhou Zhiping routinely purchased oil for the lamp at a local market.

On the fateful day, there was no way Joline's father could have known that the container of oil he bought had been intentionally or inadvertently adulterated with kerosene. When the sun set and he lit the wick to the lamp, there was an explosion, and the house was instantly engulfed in flames. In that horrific moment, the girls were talking near the kitchen table. Suddenly, Joline realized that she was on fire and ran around the room wildly in terror. The single door to the home was blocked by flames, so she could not flee outside. She tried to climb some stairs, but collapsed from shock and exquisite pain, her legs on fire. There was no immediate way to douse the flames, as the house had no running water. A few neighbors saw the blaze and attempted to put it out with blankets and buckets of water from a nearby well.

When the fire was finally contained after surreal minutes, Zhou Zhiping carried his semi-conscious daughter in his arms to a tiny local hospital. She had third-degree burns covering her hands, legs, feet, and lower abdomen. The modest clinic demanded money before agreeing to treat the girl, but the severity of her burns was beyond the facility's capacity to provide the care she needed. Zhou Zhiping managed to obtain the use of a van and drove Joline to a larger regional hospital, arriving in the middle of the night. There, over the next two months, she underwent painful surgeries, some conducted with minimal anesthesia, to amputate her severely burned fingers and toes. When it appeared that the hospital had little else to offer and the family's debts were accumulating, Joline's parents brought her back to their village. Her feet were so badly damaged that walking was out of the question, and she had very limited use of her severely burned hands.

Almost everything in the interior of the home had been destroyed by the fire. A few pieces of furniture that were usable were sold to pay off the debts from the hospital, but the building itself was still standing, and the family made do. Joline was unable to sit up due to contracting scar tissue in her back, and on the occasions when an opportunity arose to go to school, she was physically carried back and forth by her father.

For unbearable weeks, Joline cried day and night from pain, exhaustion, and despair. She was reduced to lying on her belly for extended periods in excruciating distress, trying not to think about the terrible reality of her situation: she was now a disabled girl in a culture that cruelly assigned little value to people with disabilities, especially if they were female.

Joline suffered through two months of nearly constant anguish before the family decided to make the journey to Beijing, over one thousand miles away, an arduous undertaking on rutted dirt roads. They did not own a car, so they either walked or took buses. Their primary goal was to seek justice for what had happened to Joline and Zhou Jing.

Their parents hoped to convince the Chinese government to issue a warrant to arrest the fuel dealer and, hopefully, obtain financial compensation from him or from the government. Clearly, they would need money in the future for Joline's ongoing care. The family also hoped that their daughter might qualify for additional treatment at a trauma center in the city, but they knew that the hospital would likely require payment up front. And halfway through the journey, they were nearly out of money, forcing them to stay in abandoned houses, barns, or the cheapest hotels. They traveled mostly by bus, forced to beg for the fares or by appealing to the compassion of the drivers.

Amazingly, the family found a government agent in Beijing who listened to their story. The official did, in fact, issue a complaint against the fuel dealer, but the family would later learn that the man had fled, and the chances of any compensation from him were nil. By panhandling during the day, the family was able to afford a tiny room on the outskirts of Beijing with two cardboard beds for sleeping.

The second part of the family's plan was to visit the state-run television station in the city, hoping to convince someone there to do a human-interest piece on Joline that might stir up curiosity about her case and even produce a source of financial assistance. On a frigid January morning, Joline, her mother, and her father located the station in a skyscraper in the Beijing business district. For eight days, however, they were put off, forced to huddle outside in the cold, before finally being allowed to present their idea to a junior official. The man summarily dismissed them, indicating that the station's leadership was not interested in Joline's plight.

The disheartened family gathered on the icy sidewalk outside the building, their hopes dashed. Their funds were gone, they were exhausted physically and emotionally, and hope for assistance was vanishing. Crestfallen, they resorted to panhandling outside the building in the frigid Beijing winter, seemingly out of options.

In those disheartening moments, Joline's spirit "tuned out." The unrelenting combination of pain, shock, and frustration had completely dulled her consciousness, and she had little awareness of what was going on around her. In her soul, she had essentially given up hope. She sat apathetically on a blanket, too emotionally depleted to even cry.

At that moment, high up in the building, a young American graduate student named Brecken Swartz, a PhD candidate at the University of Maryland, was in a studio working on a public service announcement. When she finished working, the brown-haired woman with a face that radiated kindness left the building and hurried down the sidewalk toward another appointment. In what would be a life-altering moment in time, she saw a beautiful, but visibly disfigured girl shivering on a blanket and stopped.

Brecken made eye contact with Joline, then bent down and touched her scarred hands, asking, "What happened to you?" They could not communicate fluently due to a difference in dialects (Brecken spoke Mandarin, while the family spoke a provincial dialect), but Joline appeared to understand when Brecken looked into her eyes and said, in English, "I will help you."

She gave the family a business card with her name on it and promised to return the next day. At dusk, gathering the small amount of money they had collected from panhandling, the family returned to the rented room. The significance of meeting Brecken did not initially dawn on Joline. She was too withdrawn to recognize that a chance meeting with an American stranger might be the turning point in her life.

Brecken, on the other hand, would later write, "My life changed in that moment."

Two years earlier, on the day of the fire, Brecken Swartz was seven thousand miles away, an excited student rushing to class to start her doctoral program at the University of Maryland. Her field was Asian Studies, an interdisciplinary program combining humanities, social sciences, and language studies focused on the Far East. Those interests were highly unusual for a young woman who grew up in rural Texas, but Brecken's fascination with Asian cultures started there during early childhood. As a little girl, she repeatedly experienced vivid dreams populated by intriguing people with straight black hair and eyes shaped differently than any she had seen in her town. She would wake up with an intense curiosity about who those people were.

By any measure, Brecken became an extraordinary scholar. As an undergraduate student at Colorado College, she went to Japan on an exchange program and passionately absorbed that culture's focus on community, respect, and harmony. As a grad student at Harvard, where she mastered Korean and Mandarin, she was exposed to Buddhism, Judaism, and Islam. She began to believe that a part of her own calling on earth would be to lessen human suffering, even if that meant assisting just a small number of people. She embraced the idea, shared by the Talmud and the Quran, that helping another human being is akin to helping all mankind. She loved the gentle parables in contemporary writings like *Winnie the Pooh* and the *Starfish Story.*

Two years after the explosion in Joline's *keekwilee,* the final piece of Brecken's study plan found her in Beijing, teaching English to Chinese students and completing research for her thesis. She was intrigued by the power of the media and had begun to consider the idea of becoming a radio producer. Interacting with journalists at the Beijing television station was part of her study plan.

True to her word, Brecken returned to the sidewalk below the studio the day after meeting Joline. She went to a nearby tearoom with Joline's father, where a stranger was able to translate between their dialects. In that café, she heard Joline's story for the first time. Brecken offered the family $200 from a grant she managed and went back outside to visit with Joline. She was about to return to the United States to complete her PhD program, but she promised that she would find a way to stay in touch. If there was anything Brecken could do to help, she vowed to do it. The family returned to their village, and Brecken flew back home.

Years later, in an interview with *People Magazine*, when asked about the chance meeting with Joline, Brecken said, "I loved her from the beginning."

About a month after Brecken returned to the US, serendipity again changed the course of two lives. Brecken was attending a hot air balloon event in New Mexico for a story she was writing when she happened upon some executives from a Shriners Hospital, the medical system known for its exceptional care for burned children. Brecken pressed them for information and quickly became convinced that she could persuade a Shriners facility to take Joline as a patient. A plan began taking shape in her head.

Communication between Brecken and the family was erratic due to the lack of phone and internet technology in rural China. Eventually, through one of Joline's cousins, a local teacher managed to get in touch with Brecken via email. The task of getting Joline to America was complicated, involving visa applications and convoluted arrangements with the Chinese government, but Brecken was making progress. She was in touch with a burn specialist, Dr. Rob Sheridan, at Shriners Hospital in Boston, who agreed to care for the child, and stunningly, Brecken learned that care at Shriners Hospitals is free.

When the teacher shared Brecken's dramatic update with Joline's parents, they elected not to share the plan with their daughter right away. They feared she would be bitterly disappointed if Brecken's scheme did not come to fruition.

Joline languished in bed for the better part of a year while Brecken worked out the arrangements. There was still no direct way for the Chinese girl to communicate with the American woman who had said, "I will help you." Then, on an early spring day with the sweet hint of plum blossoms in the air, Joline's dad announced that they were going to visit a passport office. When his daughter asked, "What for?" the time had come to reveal Brecken's plan.

At first, Joline did not believe that she might be going to America. The idea simply did not seem real. But on June 5, 2005, Joline touched down in Boston on an American Airlines flight with her mother and the teacher. She was now fourteen years old. She had carried a bouquet of flowers for Brecken all the way from Shanghai. When she was wheeled down the jetway at Logan Airport in Boston at one o'clock in the morning, Brecken was waiting at the gate.

When Joline saw Brecken's beaming face, she smiled for the first time in three years.

Brecken had raised money for a small apartment near the hospital, so the travelers from China had a place to stay while Joline was introduced to the staff at Shriners. Dr. Sheridan and his colleagues initially focused their attention on Joline's feet, concluding that amputation was necessary because there was very little healthy tissue below the ankles. If Joline wanted to walk with prosthetics someday, that draconian step would be necessary. Of course, this was unnerving news, but when she saw a little boy *running* on prosthetics down a corridor at Shriners, she understood that it was the right choice.

Shriners' motto is "Love to the Rescue." When Joline was wheeled into Shriners, she was stunned by the kindness shown to her by everyone—not just the nurses and doctors, but the administrators and the therapists. Even the custodians and an occasional visiting Shriner in his tasseled purple fez hat greeted her warmly. It had not been that way in China, not at all. Years later, when asked about the kindness she encountered at Shriners, Joline said, "I have no words that can describe how that made me feel."

Describing the difference in attitudes between China and the US regarding a disabled girl, Joline said, "It's about the culture. Cruelty is an accepted way to treat people with disabilities in China." Lying on a blanket on the frigid sidewalk in Beijing, when the family resorted to panhandling, some strangers had literally scowled at Joline and said, "You are worthless." In China, there were very few wheelchairs or accommodations for people with disabilities. The attitude there toward girls like Joline was profoundly dehumanizing, not unlike the treatment of the Dalits (*the untouchables*) in India.

Joline was undernourished when she arrived in Boston, and an initial challenge for the hospital team was to make sure her tissues were healthy enough to tolerate the anticipated surgical procedures. Her nutritionist began a program of vigorous oral supplements and protein drinks. The therapists were on standby, waiting to design and fit her prosthetic feet.

While working on a project at Shriners, I was lucky to meet Brecken and Joline not long after their arrival in the city. As I peeked in through the door of Joline's room, I felt an aura of love that both enveloped them and radiated outward from them like an energy field. The pair exuded a sense of optimism that filled the sterile hospital room. Brecken had dropped everything in her life to care for

Joline. It was astonishing to see how absolutely she adored this beautiful child who, until recently, had been a total stranger.

When I met Joline that day, she was in a wheelchair. After a month at Shriners, she used a walker when she and Brecken visited my nearby office at Massachusetts General Hospital. And then, early on a warm summer day, she appeared at our clinic door walking by herself on her new prosthetics—and she was wearing flip-flops!

I was taken aback and marveled for a moment at the astonishing care and equally astonishing kindness that Dr. Sheridan and all the therapists at Shriners had provided to Joline. Her greatest hope up to that point had been to walk again, and now she was doing it! And the bill for those months of impeccable care at Shriners? There was no bill.

At that time, Joline's mother, Guo Chunmei, needed to return to China from Boston, where her third child, now a toddler, needed her attention. Brecken was scheduled to return to China, too, for a teaching assignment, but elected instead to stay in Boston with Joline. The focus now was on improving the functionality of Joline's hands. Again, Dr. Sheridan and the therapists at Shriners did remarkable work, giving Joline the best possible result.

In early September, my twelve-year-old son, Graham, and I invited Brecken and Joline to join some campers and counselors from Camp Jabberwocky at a Harvard football game. They had spent the better part of three months inside hospital walls, and it was thrilling to see them enjoying the outdoors on a sparkling early fall day in New England. It was also fun to see the Jabberwocky campers and Joline interacting, despite the differences in their cultures and varying communication abilities. At one point, I took orders for snacks from the concession stand. Most of the campers asked for a hot dog. When I asked Joline what she would like, she innocently replied, "I'll take the turnip soup."

Later in the fall, Joline was well enough to join Brecken on a trip to Maryland to visit and meet her husband, Bill, a scientist. The visit turned into an invitation to stay for Thanksgiving, and Joline met Brecken's father and several other family members. For some time, behind the scenes, Bill and Brecken had been discussing adopting Joline. They had, in fact, already presented the idea to Joline's biological parents in China for their thoughts. Even before meeting Joline, Brecken had always hoped to have a daughter someday. She and Bill had intense discussions about the ethics and practicality of what they were considering. If Joline returned to China, she would be relegated to essentially *untouchable* status, but she would be with her biological family. If she stayed in America, loved as a daughter by Brecken and Bill, there would be opportunities for education, career, self-sufficiency, and a better quality of life.

One night after dinner, Bill and Brecken waited for the right moment and told Joline that they wanted to adopt her, leaving the final decision up to her. The proposal astonished Joline, who had been expecting to return soon to China. Suddenly, she was confronted with a life-changing decision. She stayed up all night in Brecken and Bill's guest room, thinking about the pros and cons. At the breakfast table the next morning, she smiled self-consciously and announced that she would like to become Bill and Brecken's "American daughter."

Until then, Joline's focus had been to simply walk again. She had not given much thought to the possibility of an education or a career. Accordingly, a few weeks later, she was, understandably, a bit giddy when she found herself enrolled in ninth grade at Eleanor Roosevelt High School in Greenbelt, Maryland. It was at that time that Brecken and Bill suggested Americanizing Zhou Lin to *Joline,* to make pronouncing her name easier for teachers and classmates. Following some understandable culture shock, Joline turned her attention to her studies and set a goal for herself of "getting straight As."

Her suboptimal command of English required working hard every night after school. Brecken and Bill meticulously went over every lesson with her at the kitchen table. Joline quickly realized she was very good at math and, for fun, she even took a piano class during her first year in school, using an adaptive device. A music therapist had given her some instruction in the dulcimer at Shriners, using a similar tool. Managing in school became easier after that first year, and she continued to improve her command of the English language.

Overall, Joline's experience in high school at Eleanor Roosevelt was a happy one, although she found it hard to make friends. Brecken encouraged her to pursue social activities outside the home, but she was understandably self-conscious. The other kids did not snub her, but socializing was intimidating.

Two years later, Brecken received a job offer to become a junior professor at Curry College, near Boston. An important benefit in her mind was free tuition for faculty children, both at Curry and its sister school, Dean College, located in nearby Franklin, Massachusetts. Brecken hoped that Joline would become more engaged with classmates in college, and she did, choosing Dean because the campus grounds were physically easier for her, and the atmosphere there seemed more supportive.

Neither Joline's Chinese heritage nor her disability led to bullying or unkind behavior from the students at Dean. Still, she remained cautious around the other students because of the cultural differences and her use of prosthetics. She did well in art and business classes and wondered for a time about a career in architecture. She gradually became more social and even joined some social clubs at Dean.

After graduation, Joline found a part-time job in a small company near her home in Maryland, before starting a full-time position as an office manager and event planner in Alexandria, Virginia. She tested the waters with dating, but nothing serious developed. When Brecken and Bill divorced when Joline was twenty-one, she was disappointed, but took the development in stride. From time to time, she spent time with her "American grandparents" in Pennsylvania and Texas.

Joline communicated by phone and FaceTime with her family in China on a weekly basis. She made trips to China in 2009, 2019, and 2023. Her "Chinese family" was always astonished at her progress and intensely proud of her. For her part, Joline was amazed at the economic development in her old community. There seemed to be change everywhere, and it was hard to even recognize her old village. Her dad, a farmer all his life, was now working in an office. Joline recalled being told that when her mother was a child, girls were treated so disrespectfully that they were not even allowed to sit at the dinner table with the rest of the family. While there is still gender prejudice in China today, Joline and her childhood "tail," her younger sister Zhou Jing, are college graduates now and symbols of progress.

Building on the experience with Joline, Brecken and some colleagues started HandReach, a small nonprofit dedicated to bringing additional Chinese youngsters with severe burns to America for physical and emotional care at Shriners. The group raised some money and got to work. A question among the staff at HandReach has been whether Joline will one day take over the leadership of the program. At this moment, she is not sure. She likes her work as a project manager and is financially self-sufficient. She has a few close friends. With adaptations to her car, she drives herself to work and back. She is very proud of what she has accomplished. She is happy. Joline will decide about HandReach when the time is right.

Postscript

Tragically, Brecken passed away suddenly while visiting China in 2019. The cause of her death was never known definitively. The grieving staff at HandReach released this post quoting Mary Baker Eddy: "When angels visit us, we do not hear the rustle of wings, nor feel the feathery touch of the breast of a dove; but we know their presence by the love they create in our hearts."

After the tragedy, Joline wrote this about the woman who saved her life:

"Brecken and I loved each other. Our connection was shaped by a mutual hope that the other felt supported, truly understood and free. The bond we shared was rooted in an unspoken understanding of each other's hearts."

SERIOUSLY SILLY

The Down Syndrome guys from Momeraths, along with a few from JubJub, were enjoying a belly laugh at my expense. Will Halby, who had provoked them, hid behind the table where they sat finishing breakfast, giggling mischievously. As I stood self-consciously at one end of the main cabin, solemnly preparing to remind the eighty or so campers and counselors of Camp Jabberwocky about the importance of hand washing, a derisive chorus of "Doctor Steve, Doctor Steve, Doctor Steve!" drowned me out entirely.

As I attempted to restart the dry presentation, the rest of the campers and counselors joined in, and the walls of the old building echoed raucously with the chant. With a third round of "Doctor Steve, Doctor Steve, Doctor Steve!" ringing in my ears, I began to feel like a New York Yankee hitter stepping up to the plate at Fenway Park amid a deafening serenade of mocking insults from the Red Sox faithful.

Well, no. I knew that this heckling was different. Will, a veteran counselor, and the campers at the breakfast table to my left, lovingly known at Camp Jabberwocky as "the Downies," were simply having some fun with me. That whimsical outburst of abuse was, paradoxically, their way of welcoming me into the Jabberwocky family.

Looking around that modest room, surrounded by uninhibited grins, my self-consciousness dissolved. I experienced, in fact, a glowing awareness that these people genuinely cared about me. As the laughter dissipated, I knew that I now officially belonged to the Jabberwocky family. I had just been initiated into a community where, as our camp director loves to say, "We take our silliness very seriously."

A markedly different environment awaited me a month later when I reluctantly left the haven of the Jabberwocky campus on Martha's Vineyard and resumed my career as an internist at a Boston teaching hospital. Getting to the medical center was a "pick your poison" proposition from my home north of the city, and I generally chose the lesser evil of commuting by train. On my first day back, I waited on a windy platform in the predawn gloom with roughly a hundred other souls who worked in the city. During the month that I had been at Jabberwocky, I had forgotten just how demoralizing the trip into the city could be.

As our train screeched to a halt, I watched sullen people pushing aggressively toward the door of the nearest car. They were aware that, when all the seats on the train are occupied, stragglers can end up standing all the way to North Station. The cars on our commuter line have rows with three seats on either side of a center aisle. Few people enjoy the middle seat, where you can become uncomfortably intimate with the sounds and scents of your neighbors. But, for most of the travelers, a middle seat still beats standing.

Owing to the absence of college students, there tend to be fewer riders in July and August, and on the morning of my return, the middle seats were initially empty. The COVID-19 pandemic had not yet descended upon us, but, as if anticipating one, the people sitting on the aisles and windows were glumly maximizing the distance between one another.

As we stopped at the handful of stations en route to the city, demand for the middle spots slowly increased, and I observed a familiar tableau. The occupants of the aisle seats were focusing so intently on their electronic devices that they seemed to have lost their peripheral vision. They appeared to be entirely oblivious to the fellow travelers standing in the aisle right next to them. Even a young woman, vividly close to the end of pregnancy, was somehow invisible to those morose people. When specifically approached by one of the standers, the keepers of the aisle seats—looking greatly put upon—would stand up. With unconcealed looks of exasperation, they would grudgingly yield the middle seats next to them that had previously been home to their coffee mugs and backpacks.

During the thirty-minute ride, it seemed to me that no two people in the entire car made eye contact, nor was a single laugh or giggle audible. The overall impression was that of a collection of people on a forced march to an unpleasant destiny. A downtrodden lot they were, and by the time we reached North Station, I had begun to feel a little downtrodden myself.

Waiting for the passengers to gather their things and disembark, I had a couple of minutes to contemplate the resigned misery and general air of suffering that seemed to characterize the passengers on my train. I recalled a Stanford University study from a few years earlier that observed that babies laugh three hundred times per day, compared with twenty times for adults. One researcher described this as a "laughter cliff," which most of us fall off in our early twenties, just about the time we enter the workforce.

During a break at work, I decided to look up the Stanford study. Humor, it said, creates bonding among co-workers and facilitates creativity and collaboration. Laughing reduces tension and lowers the stress hormone cortisol while elevating the "feel good" hormone oxytocin. So why is it, I wondered, that so many commuters and office workers seem to take their seriousness so seriously?

Shaking off the gloom of my commute, I felt powerfully grateful for my time at Camp Jabberwocky. Being in a place where you have laughed heartily with people who care about you turns out to be a gift that can be transferred across space and time, a phenomenon that Ernest Hemingway called a "movable feast." In addition, according to the Stanford group, simply recalling joyful times, like my month at Jabberwocky, actually creates hormonal changes in real time that are essentially identical to those that occurred during the experiences themselves.

Considering all this, I resolved to try a simple strategy going forward should I find myself having a bad day at work: Shut the door, close my eyes, take a few slow breaths, and listen for the affectionately mocking cheers I received from Will and the Downies—a bit of serious silliness that will always restore my smile.

THE LIGHTKEEPER

"Let the celebration of all our children
And their endless youth
When the world was to them still without problem
Always be that unforgotten Vineyard summer
An everlasting day."

—Tomas Napolean

At the mouth of Edgartown Harbor, on a crescent-shaped sand bar created by the Great New England Hurricane of 1938, a simple white lighthouse stands proudly above shallow, windswept dunes.

Feathery beach grasses, outwardly delicate but rooted with enormous strength, bind those dunes against the shifting sands of the tiny peninsula that faces Chappaquiddick Island, just a few hundred yards across the channel.

The Edgartown Lighthouse sits serenely in that place, at the confluence of winding sandy paths bordered by wild New England beach roses, which fragrantly display their vibrant pink blossoms every summer. Around the foundation of that lighthouse rests a memorial made of granite cobblestones containing the names of children "whose lives were cut short by untimely deaths."

On one of those stones is the name "Graham Hale Gardner."

Rick Harrington, a lifelong Vineyard resident and father of one of the children remembered there, conceived of the memorial and nurtured it into being. The steward of the memorial today is the Martha's Vineyard Museum, while the lighthouse itself, with its flashing red beacon, remains an active aid to the navigation of the US Coast Guard.

The Children's Lighthouse Memorial was created "with the fervent hope that for the families of these children, whose interrupted lives are here remembered, that this lighthouse be a beacon through the darkness of grief, reminding and assuring us all with its brightness that a safe harbor has indeed been reached."

It was Graham's mother, Cynthia, who discovered this singular place of remembrance and arranged Graham's inclusion in it. His place of honor there was Cynthia's surprise Christmas gift to me at the end of our first year without him. A kindly stonemason named Dudley Levick set the piece of granite with Graham's name on it in the ground in that lustrous place on the magnificent island that had meant so much to all three of us.

Cynthia spotted Dudley working there shortly after she arrived on the island in the summer of 2010, his bright blue eyes sparkling behind rimmed glasses, sweating from the effort of his task. Ruddy-faced beneath a tattered straw hat, he was kneeling at the center of a pile of cobblestones, meticulously setting the last pieces of the memorial in place.

Cynthia watched him place a granite marker in the sandy ground with quiet reverence. She bent down to thank him and shared some photos of our son, so that Dudley could picture the boy whose stone (and memory) he had handled with such care.

A few days later, on a brilliant summer morning while I was across the island at Camp Jabberwocky, Cynthia walked out to the lighthouse to visit the finished memorial for the first time, acutely aware that she was approaching a hallowed place. She was met in the arched doorway of the lighthouse tower by a slender man with beautiful coffee-colored skin. He was singing and greeting visitors as if he were welcoming them into his own home. Cynthia was further amazed to hear the celestial sounds of an aria reverberating within the conical belly of the lighthouse.

Wade Johnson introduced himself and said he was the keeper of the lighthouse and also an overseer of the monument. He considered himself, too, a caretaker for the spirits of the children memorialized there. It was instantly clear to Cynthia that, for Wade, this was indeed a sacred place. She watched him for several minutes as he carefully and kindly explained the history of the memorial to a steady stream of visitors. She was deeply moved by the kind, spiritual man and his singular devotion to the task he had been given.

A few days later, Cynthia and I walked to the lighthouse together on a sandy path from North Water Street. It was my first visit to the memorial, and I felt my emotions rising. As we neared the structure, my senses became aware of something serene. It took me a couple of moments to realize that it was the music coming from inside the forty-five-foot-high cast iron tower.

I spotted Wade inside the door and wondered if Gandhi had come back to life! The slim, graceful lightkeeper was wearing a T-shirt that featured images of all the lighthouses on the island. He gave me a warm welcome that seemed to embrace my entire being and walked me over to Graham's stone, where Cynthia was spreading wild rose petals. It was both shocking and beautiful to see Graham's name there.

Wade stood with us quietly. We spoke of Graham, and I had the curious feeling that he had something to share about our son that even his parents may not have known.

Wade looked into my eyes and said, "Graham's mission was complete."

Cynthia and I were lucky to spend a little time that morning with that gentle man. It was a relatively quiet day with only a few tourists requiring his attention. Wade explained his conviction that the spirits of the memorialized children were present right there in that place of stunning beauty where land and sea meet in such harmony. As I listened, I began to appreciate that there was a double meaning to Wade's title of "lightkeeper."

While Wade monitored the structure of the lighthouse and its beacon, it was clear that he intended to do his part to keep the light alive that Graham had shone on this world, along with the spirits of all the other children whose names would forever sit at the base of that beautiful tower. Wade explained that part of his mission was to welcome every visitor into this special place of light and urge them to "touch, smell, and see."

Cynthia and I wanted all of Camp Jabberwocky to share in this experience and arranged for the visit about a week later. On the appointed day, the campers and counselors arrived en masse, pushing and pulling wheelchairs laboriously but excitedly down one of the sandy paths. Wade welcomed everyone in his characteristically calm, easy fashion and explained the history and mission of the memorial. Then, he answered questions, with all of the campers fanned out in a half circle around him in the sand at the base of the lighthouse.

At that moment, I was standing on the outside walk of the lantern room at the top of the lighthouse tower, looking straight down at Wade as he addressed Camp Jabberwocky. Those special people—campers and counselors whose lives were marked by kindness, resilience, and pure joy—had loved Graham and still did. Along with Graham, they had transformed how I see the world.

In response to a question from a camper about the memorial, I heard Wade say, "The souls of these children are always communicating. Some of us can hear them, and some cannot. The souls here at the base of the lighthouse are spiritual donors sending energy to those who go to the top and look out onto the world. There is healing in that for us all. The light that shines here is a celebration of life."

I could see Graham's stone off to the northeast side of the monument in my peripheral vision. Surrounded by an unbroken view of natural harmony, I knew I was witnessing something that I might never experience again.

When Wade finished speaking, naturally, everyone from camp wanted to climb the spiral stairs inside the lighthouse to the spectacular platform above. The view from that circular landing offers "a sense of how magnificent the world is—or should be," as Wade put it.

But visitors must ascend the last seven feet on a vertical ladder to reach the breathtaking "gallery" at the top, where I was standing. I doubted that any visitor in a wheelchair had ever made it up that vertical ladder all the way to the platform in the history of the lighthouse.

But, of course! It never even occurred to the Jabberwocky counselors that they couldn't or shouldn't assist campers in wheelchairs all the way up that ladder and out onto the glorious platform with its stunning panorama of the harbor and the village of Edgartown. In another Jabberwocky epiphany, I watched the counselors carry campers up the vertical wall and out to the rarified place where they could savor the breathtaking views in every direction.

In time, the campers and counselors descended, found their way to the side of the lighthouse where Graham's stone sat within the polished granite border of the memorial, and paused there, quietly remembering him.

Camp had brought a picnic, and all we had to do was walk another thirty yards or so past the memorial, and we were ready for a day at the beach, with the bonus of watching a parade of boats sailing in and out of the harbor.

Later, as the counselors pulled their campers back to town along the sandy path, I spotted Wade smiling at me from the doorway of the lighthouse and, for a moment, the world seemed without problem. An unforgettable moment in a Vineyard summer.

An everlasting day.

Over time, I was lucky enough to become Wade's friend, and I gradually learned about the improbable journey that brought him to the lighthouse and memorial in Edgartown.

He grew up in a bustling "three-decker" multi-generational home in Roxbury, Massachusetts, the modest Black neighborhood on the southern edge of Boston. His mom, Shirley, was just sixteen when Wade was born, and he was only thirteen when his father was murdered. His grandfather earned a living tending bar while his grandmother kept a close eye on Wade, his brother Benjamin, and half-sister Karla.

Wade's granddad was "obsessed" with the importance of education, and Shirley was among the first Black women to attend the Boston University School of Nursing. The critical importance of schooling was instilled early on in Wade, and he was even finagled into kindergarten a year early. In time, the family managed to move from Roxbury to nearby Newton, an affluent, largely white suburb with excellent schools. After an understandably unnerving transitional period, Wade held his own there academically and socially.

When Wade and I first talked about his childhood, it suddenly dawned on me that at the time he was playing sandlot baseball in Roxbury, I was doing exactly the same—on the manicured little league fields of the leafy Boston suburb of Weston, only twelve miles away as the crow flies, but a galaxy away in just about every other way. When I revealed to Wade that I had been raised in that country club environment, he responded this way, without envy or self-pity: "While you were in the business of thriving, I was in the business of surviving."

Wade did very well at Newton South High School, and with the encouragement of his guidance counselor and support from the United States Senator from Massachusetts, Edward Brooke, an African American, he applied to the elite Williams College and was accepted.

On the much-anticipated day of his college matriculation, Wade would have been justified to feel like a stranger in a strange land, a Martian falling out of the sky through the brilliant fall foliage of the Berkshire Mountains in western Massachusetts—and touching down in one of New England's rarefied pinnacles of social privilege and academic distinction.

As if adjusting to the stately Romanesque buildings there—a far cry from the ramshackle three-decker in Roxbury—was not sufficient culture shock, a Black Panther group on campus quickly commenced efforts to radicalize Wade's young mind, trying to make him feel guilty for not being "Black enough."

"They wanted to *chocklafy* me—to convince me that white people are devils," Wade recalled.

Said one of the *brothers*: "Your blackness got bleached out of you, man!"

And, up to a point, Wade did relate to that nascent movement of racial pride and economic empowerment that was emerging on campuses across the country. But, at the same time, his heart told him that, in an intellectual and cultural haven like Williams, he had been given a rare opportunity to connect with people from *all* backgrounds and to learn from them. He was ready to feel the energy of the entire universe, not partition it into solar systems divided by color or any other superficial label.

Thinking about Wade in that early crucible, my brain suddenly pictured him as Odysseus, navigating his way between the equally formidable perils of Scilla and Charybdis, dodging their hideous heads, baying dogs, and sucking whirlpools.

But, no. As it turned out, Wade did not find his circumstances in Williamstown excessively intimidating at all, and he traversed the curious gauntlet between white preppies and Black Panthers rather easily, refusing to define himself in anyone else's terms. After all, he had experience in that area, having made his way confidently as a Black kid in the privileged air of the elite schools back in Newton.

And beyond the understandable culture shock, the preppies, and the brothers, there was an even more powerful force exerting its influence on the young man every day. It was Shirley—so intensely proud of her boy and so deeply concerned about him—that she aggressively cross-examined him at length on the phone at night about his decision-making and how he was handling all the new demands on his intellect and spirit.

As the dust settled on his transition to Williams, Wade did just fine socially and academically. But when an opportunity arose to participate in a pioneering exchange program with the historically female Vassar College in Poughkeepsie, New York, he jumped at the opportunity and launched himself without hesitation into another brave new world. The 1,500 scholarly women there looked upon him not with suspicion or resentment, but with something more like healthy curiosity. He thrived in their midst, eventually becoming an admissions officer and assisting the school with the challenge of bringing minority men into what had been a rarefied female enclave for more than a century.

At Vassar, Wade discovered a love for psychology and he explored not just Black history, but the history of a variety of other cultures. As I listened to this part of his story one day, I developed a funny image of my friend as a kind of "cultural astronaut," fearlessly steering his innate humanism and curiosity into "strange new worlds," like the captain of the Starship Enterprise.

After graduating cum laude with dual degrees in Black Studies and Psychology from Vassar, Wade enrolled in a pioneering school in Brattleboro, Vermont, a place referred to as "the Experiment in International Living," or simply "The Experiment." The bucolic campus there was among the first settings for the training of Peace Corps volunteers. Its lofty mission of promoting understanding across cultures was rapidly coming into focus as Wade's own sphere of interest.

"The Experiment" offered workshops and internships off campus, and the young seeker of wisdom accepted an opportunity to explore that emerging field at an innovative program in Canada.

In Ontario, Wade continued to seek out his own personal identity while working with several government offices on issues relating to human rights and cultural affairs. He attended a residential retreat called a "peace camp" at a place named Grindstone Island, an eleven-acre sanctuary in a body of water aptly called Big Riddle Lake. He described his time there as a "kind of Tarot deck of an experience," contemplating the planet's future while trying to fathom what he called the "*human wrong* in *human rights*."

Eventually, Wade returned to Boston and worked at Mount Ida College for a while before joining the guidance department in the Cape Cod village of Barnstable. At that time, Shirley lived on the nearby island of Martha's Vineyard, where Wade had a connection in the school system. Following a period of reflection, he boarded a steamship in Falmouth, crossed the six miles of shimmering cobalt blue water called Nantucket Sound, and prepared to start his life anew.

He landed a job in the copy center at the regional school on the island where he was immediately recognized for creating an "emotional oasis" for the students. The little office became a kind of sanctuary where the island's budding scholars could talk to Wade about anything on their minds. The job was fine. Until, one day after work, while reading the *Vineyard Gazette* newspaper, an advertisement caught his attention—the stewards of the Edgartown Lighthouse were looking for a lightkeeper.

In that moment, Wade Barry Johnson could not have known that, on that picturesque island dotted with fields of wildflowers, his destiny awaited. His arrival at the Edgartown Lighthouse and Memorial would turn out to be nothing less than "the end to which he was born."

After a lifetime of spiritual exploration, a singular journey that carried a callow boy with coffee-colored skin from the gritty streets of Roxbury to the windy shores of Big Riddle Lake in Canada, Wade had arrived at the apotheosis of his career. The purpose for which God had put him on this earth was literally in the wind there—on a sand bar at the entrance to one of the most breathtaking harbors in the world.

Wade might object to this term, but the lessons that ultimately revealed themselves on that breezy barrier beach became for him a kind of *ministry.* He was not a preacher in the literal sense, pressing a theme to a passive congregation within a church, synagogue, or temple. But his domain—the serene space in and around the lighthouse—was perhaps a bit like a Quaker meeting house, a setting where visitors could quietly contemplate ideas that Wade encouraged them to consider.

In that place of awe-inspiring physical beauty, at the majestic confluence of land and sea, Wade Johnson gave visitors the chance to pause and "listen for God."

As the years passed under his watch, the radiance of the children remembered there never dimmed. Wade dedicated himself to "lifting the pain" of mourning families, delivering on the Memorial's promise of offering them a "beacon through the darkness of grief." In addition, he always encouraged his guests to slow down and absorb the singularly serene setting around them, a place some people now consider to be sacred.

"I was sent out there to do those things," he told me, referring not to the supportive people who had hired him at the Martha's Vineyard Museum, the steward of the memorial, but to a much more ethereal source of inspiration. Among Wade's gentle messages to all who approached was the notion that Graham and the other children remembered there belong to *all* of us. They are *our* children. And we are *all* connected.

Wade then shared a vivid exchange he had with a five-year-old African-American boy who visited the memorial while vacationing on the island with his family. After running excitedly toward the lighthouse, the youngster had gazed up with an apprehensive expression at the big tower. Probably remembering a horror movie that had scared him, the boy asked Wade if the lighthouse was haunted.

"Yes, it is!" replied the lightkeeper. "It's haunted by some very wonderful souls who want to share their beautiful energy with you."

For several minutes, the child silently walked around the memorial with his family, staring intently at the names etched in the stones. Then, with a look of wonderment on his face, the boy looked up keenly at Wade. Pointing to a stone near the base of the tower, he said, "She wants to tell her family that she loves them."

On a crisp fall morning at a diner called the Katama Kitchen, Wade and I talked at length about the lighthouse and memorial over French toast and coffee.

"That place washed my soul," he remarked, as we watched a young mother tenderly holding her baby on an adjacent picnic table. "It was as if the world came to my doorstep."

Philosophical musings typically pop out of Wade's mouth without apparent thought, like popcorn from a microwave. From time to time, I have fun provoking him with unanswerable existential questions. So, after a pause in our conversation about the memorial, I asked Wade for his thoughts about a much less pleasant subject, the seemingly insurmountable tensions that exist among human beings based on differences in culture, religion, and skin color.

Without apparent thought, he replied, "I don't believe in black and white. I believe in what is *in between*. I could not care less about a person's skin color. We all bleed red. The only thing that matters is what is within the heart."

"Okay, Wade, but there is so much divisiveness in the world today. Not too long ago, I remember talking about the country and, even the world, becoming a 'kinder, gentler place.' Clearly, that has not happened."

"For some reason, a lot of people in the world today are ready to do battle with one another. Most of them are afraid of something. And many are just lonely, wondering where they belong, like Eleanor Rigby."

"That said, you lifted the pain of many people at the Memorial, Wade."

"Well, what can I really give to society? For me, the most important thing I do is listen. I always ask, 'How are you? Where are you from?' Everybody has a story. It takes so little to share positive energy and lighten someone else's burden."

"Understood, but sometimes the nightly news is just so demoralizing..."

"Regardless of what is going on in the world out there, I can only be myself. That's all I can do. I *care* about people. I try to keep my light shining in hopes that it encourages other people to find and shine their own light."

My friend paused for a few moments and looked at me with a beatific smile.

"I will always be a lightkeeper."

BEST MAN

"I am struck by the sense that most of us lead a life of disability, the disability of distance and restraint. It is the one disability not in evidence at Camp Jabberwocky."

—Sarah Putnam, HOPE magazine

The summer after Graham's passing, on the first day of camp, I read alphabetically through the health histories provided by each camper at the beginning of each Jabberwocky session. I needed to refresh my memory about their medical and social issues. At the end of the thick ring-bound notebook was a file on Sam Wood, a young man with Down Syndrome I had known for a number of years.

Perhaps due to his dark beard and linebacker's build, Sam can appear gruff to someone meeting him for the first time. This gracious man, however, is about as far from gruff as a human being can be. Like many other people with the chromosomal condition called Trisomy 21, Sam's personality is characterized by a profound gentleness. Jabberwocky is always thrilled to have campers with Down Syndrome in its midst.

After reading through Sam's medical forms, I walked down to the Vineyard Haven ferry terminal with the excited, crazily dressed throng of counselors who, by tradition, greet the campers coming off the boat with flamboyant cheers and songs. One of the first campers to walk down the gangway, with an enormous smile on his face, was another camper named Sam.

Sam Stoddard was a much-loved young man with Down Syndrome. Sporting a T-shirt that said, "I have an extra chromosome and I know how to use it," Sam was followed closely by Kendra, Michaela, Skye, and still another Sam (called "Rhyno" for short, an affectionate contraction of his last name), four more campers with Down Syndrome, all cherished by everyone in the camp family.

A few moments later, Sam Wood walked carefully down the ramp and was swallowed by the loud, collective embrace of Camp Jabberwocky. In the raucous crowd at the ferry terminal, it occurred to me that the three Sams, Kendra, Michaela, and Skye indeed knew how to use their extra twenty-first chromosomes—they spread kindness and humanity in our world, although I doubt that a genetics researcher could explain that in terms of DNA sequences.

As I watched Sam Wood walk away from the ferry terminal with his counselor, I recalled a section on his health form that made me chuckle: "Loves food and will eat just about anything." I also remembered a section in which a physician had indicated that "his intellectual disability can cause slow processing time and some difficulty verbally expressing himself."

That afternoon, I sat by myself on the big porch swing outside the doors to Camp Jabberwocky's main cabin thinking about Graham and all we had experienced together at Jabberwocky. My heart was full, as it was so often in that special place. I was lost in that reverie when I noticed Sam Wood slowly approaching from the direction of his cabin. We exchanged a smile, and he quietly sat down next to me on the swing.

In a gesture that was completely natural, he rested his head gently on my left shoulder. Then, in a barely audible voice that was steady and soothing, he said, "I miss Graham. I love Graham. I love you. That will never change."

What a wonderful world it would be, I thought, *if we all had such difficulty expressing ourselves.*

One winter day, I was reminiscing with Kristen "Sully" Sullivan, a beloved director of Jabberwocky for twenty-five years, when the subject of Sam Wood came up. I had sensed over our summers together at Camp that those two shared a special bond. Sully told me that, during those madcap sessions on the island, Sam had paid her daily visits in the director's cabin when her first child, Bella, was very young.

Sam apparently sensed that Sully was a bit overwhelmed by the massive responsibility of running Jabberwocky while caring for a toddler and made it a point to stop in every day and offer his support. Within the joyous but non-stop mayhem of Jabberwocky, his peaceful presence calmed Sully. Typically, Sam would sit down on the scruffy, sagging couch in her little cabin and hold Bella or help her organize toys while Sully caught up on her many pressing duties. Before leaving, Sam would then take a few minutes to fold Sully and Bella's laundry. The friendship that blossomed among Sully, Bella, and Sam in the Jabberwocky director's cabin over many magical summers continues to grow.

Bella shared these thoughts about that special bond:

> *"I like to think I was born into the Camp family. I have attended Camp every year of my life since I was born. Over the past fourteen summers, I have met many great people, but one of the most incredible I've ever met is Sam Wood. We share a love of theatre and music. I remember watching Sam in a stage production of* Guys and Dolls *where he lit up the stage. It was amazing to see him up there in his element. Hanging out with Sam has been a unique pleasure in my life, and I enjoy getting to know him better year by year. He is an unbelievably special guy, and I'm incredibly lucky to call him my friend."*

JoJo Romero, another of Jabberwocky's beloved camp directors (over more than three decades!), reflected on her own powerful bond with Sam:

> *"Jabberwocky is all about laughter, and no one laughs deeper than Sam. He is incredibly funny, and I love playing jokes with him (and on him!). For so many summers, I have also had the great pleasure of dancing with Sam—he is always the heart of our music and choreography adventures at Camp. And Sam is also a cuddler without equal! His hugs make your heart smile and make you feel safe. Sam is an incredibly loyal soul who loves his friends and family with his full heart."*

Susie, one of Sam's exuberant friends and counselors, described running into him at Camp this way:

> *"Sam's way of saying hello each summer was always—always!—the best. He would be walking slowly along one of the Jabberwocky paths, as was his practice, and suddenly a smile would appear on his face when he'd spot you. Then he'd beckon you in for a hug and a kiss on the head. You'd never want to miss the 'I missed you' and the genuine 'How are you doing?' that would come next in his low, gravelly voice. If you were ever going through a hard time, you could count on Sam to offer a literal shoulder to lean on. He literally taught me how to be a better friend!"*

I asked Isabelle and Keenan, two more of Sam's fabulous friends and counselors over the years at Jabberwocky (and later the Camp at Ashmere), about our friend. Keenan replied with these words:

> *"Isabelle and I met as counselors at Jabberwocky in 2016, kicking off a journey that would blossom into a love story over our summers together and six years later bring us to the shores of Lake Ashmere in western Massachusetts for our 'camp wedding.' That place became extremely special for us when we helped found the Ashmere Project on its shores in 2022. The idea behind the project was to evolve off*

the Jabberwocky model and create a retreat for adults with and without disabilities, a community of friends who celebrate diversity and inclusion. Each summer, we pull out all the stops and put on a boisterous evening in our fortnight at Ashmere to celebrate an event—a birthday, a friend's achievement, something the community feels worthy of a red carpet, five-star service in the dining hall, followed by a night of dancing. In 2024, the special event was our wedding—the wedding of Isabelle and Keenan!

"The entire camp group woke up eager to make the day one to remember. The morning was spent decorating the ceremonial space on the lakefront, as well as the dining hall, the dance floor, and a tennis court behind one of the cabins. As everyone raided the costume area to put together their 'formal silly' attire, Isabelle and I were quarantined to our respective cabins to maintain an element of surprise. Sequestered and brimming with excitement for the evening ahead, we were tasked with making decisions about the wedding party. A particularly important role in all of this was someone to walk the bride down the aisle. (Isabelle's father was, in fact, present, but was saving his walk with her for the "official" wedding day later in the year.) There was no question about who this person should be. It was always Sam Wood.

"Isabelle and I had known Sam since our early days at Jabberwocky, and he had been there with us every step of the way through our journey and burgeoning

relationship. During bus rides, beach days, trips to the farm, and nights performing skits, Sam was always there with a smile on his face, a soothing demeanor, and his great bear hug. Sam has always been an observer, taking everything in and offering honest and sincere assessments of what's going on, and I always enjoy finding him amidst the camp craziness to check in and have a moment of quiet conversation. It was in one such moment that I first confided in Sam that Isabelle and I were dating. His brilliant smile and 'I love you guys! You are a great match!' that followed is something that I'll always remember.

"Flashing forward to 2024, my eyes brimmed with tears looking up the aisle and seeing Isabelle in a whimsical sequined white outfit, arm in arm with Sam in his peach blazer, white dress shirt, and pinstriped vest. As I learned later, when Isabelle acknowledged her nervousness as the ceremony approached, Sam took her arm and told her, 'Go slowly. You will be just fine. It is an honor to walk with you.'

"As they approached the altar, with the lake behind us and the sun setting on the horizon, Sam then placed his arm on my own shoulder and said, 'You take care of her,' and I promised him I would, thanking him for escorting my wife-to-be down the aisle to the beach. Sam, with tears welling in his eyes, gave me a big squeeze and said, 'I know you will.'

"He then turned and walked slowly back to his reserved seat in the front, before joining in song with

the rest of our Ashmere friends, setting the stage for a night that Isabelle and I will remember fondly for the rest of our days."

Harry, Sam's zany companion and counselor, had this to say about his friend:

"Sam is so incredibly gentle. When tense situations arose in the cabin we shared, he was unfailingly helpful. If one of the campers got mad or threw a tantrum, it was always Sam who calmed him down. We all knew that Sam could be trusted absolutely. For years, for example, one of the campers would not let anyone else shave him except Sam. In his quiet, gentle way, Sam was able to assist another camper whose OCD was causing him considerable upset in the frequently chaotic setting of Camp Jabberwocky. Sam, more than anybody else, camper or counselor, instinctively knew how to help him."

Mike, Sam's buddy and theatrical collaborator, shared these reflections from their time together at Camp Jabberwocky and Lake Ashmere:

"I always think about what a wonderful actor Sam is. He loves the theater. The first time I see him every summer, he rushes over to me and wants to

> *talk about the play, sharing his ideas on casting, character arcs, and how to create moments that let everyone shine. Two summers ago, we did* Annie, *and for the first week of camp, he insisted on playing Daddy Warbucks. But after a few days, Sam saw how many people were interested in that role, and he pulled me aside: "You know, I was thinking, I actually would make a better Rooster." (Rooster is Miss Hannigan's brother and henchman). Sam wasn't focused on having the biggest role—he wanted others to enjoy the spotlight. And he worked hard to help create memorable characters and scenes.*
>
> *"Every year, throughout the rehearsal process of that summer's play, he's encouraging and complimentary. Whenever I get stressed or nervous about us not having enough time to pull the production together, he seems to sense my emotions and always comes up to me with a hug to tell me what a wonderful job everyone is doing."*

Sam's sparkling companion and counselor, Caroline, described him this way:

> *"Sam has always been the quiet anchor of our camp community. Through his careful observation and patient listening, he brings a deep sense of comfort*

and support to all around him. He is the first to notice when someone isn't quite themselves, offering kindness in thoughtful and understated ways. I can think of countless moments when, without being asked, Sam sat beside me at dinner or gave me a big hug at exactly the right time—small gestures that meant so much to me."

Samantha, another of Sam's joyful Jabberwocky friends, summarized her feelings about him in a single sentence:

"Sam is a gentle and kind soul who instinctively spreads kindness everywhere he goes."

Jake, another buoyant Jabberwocky friend, has been close to Sam for a long time now. He told a funny story about proudly taking Sam for a long walk and being impressed by Sam's honesty afterward when Sam told him he didn't really like long walks. Jake described Sam Wood as a "supremely kind human being." Being a quasi-scientist, I asked Jake the old conundrum: was Sam's personality the result of "nature or nurture," genetics or environment? Jake is close to both Joe and Jeanine, Sam's parents, and after thinking for a few moments, he said, "Maybe it's both. God made Sam that way, but his nature was also cultivated by having amazing parents."

Sam's steadfast friend and counselor, Mara, said this about him:

> *"I have been lucky enough to be bunkmates with Sam multiple times and have always been so grateful and impressed by his incredible generosity and compassion. He is always such a total team player, doing what he can to help out the group as a whole. He is also someone who is very in touch with and perceptive about how other people are feeling. When other people may not even pick up on it, Sam can tell if someone isn't feeling their best and is the first to check in on them and offer a hug."*

Sam's dad, Joe, shared a note with me from the place where Sam works. "We call Sam the voice of reason," said a supervisor. "When other mentors bring up struggles that are going on, Sam always has a positive solution on how to handle a situation. He is unfailingly kind and willing to help whenever needed. He is a loyal friend and looks out for those he cares about."

I asked Joe how it could be that so many people view Sam this way. He replied, "Sam has an honesty which he lays bare when he speaks. What I love and appreciate about Sam is that he isn't trying. It's just the way he is."

When the campers and volunteers board the big ferry and leave the haven of Camp Jabberwocky at the end of the summer and cross the six miles of Vineyard Sound to the mainland and the "real world," many of us find ourselves asking the same question: "Why can't the *real world* be more like Camp Jabberwocky?"

When we think about the dissonance, harshness, and lack of courtesy separating so many people in the world today, many of us also find ourselves asking, "Why can't more people be like Sam Wood?"

TWO REUBENS

The old man I had met just a week earlier appeared to be crying. A tear dropped onto the toasted pumpernickel rye of his Reuben sandwich as we faced each other across a small laminated table on the sidewalk outside Larry's Lunchbox, a tiny deli in a strip mall no different than a thousand others in South Florida. At about the same time, my own eyes began to well up.

A harried waitress passed us with a look of concern, before deciding to leave well enough alone.

I had met my companion, Don Hecht, seemingly by chance between the second and third holes of a modest public golf course nearby. The builder had dubbed the place "Pelican Shores," notwithstanding the fact that it lay many miles from the nearest beach and the only birds I noticed there were crows. He probably figured that naming the place "The golf course I created by filling in a swamp with a small army of underpaid workers from Ecuador" would lack the cachet he was aiming for.

I had set off on the course by myself one afternoon, savoring some time alone. I was practicing putting on the green of the second hole, although calling it a "green" was a misnomer, its grass being more the color of moderately burned toast. It was one of those mom-and-pop courses that are prevalent in the unglamorous neighborhoods of Florida, where the ordinary people live who service the more glamorous enclaves along the beaches. At Pelican Shores, the fairways were lined with double-wide mobile homes with F-150 and Ram pick-ups protruding from carports and fluorescent Big Wheel tricycles lying on their sides next to giant gas grills. I've played at a few fancy golf clubs over the years, and they can be fine in their own way, but for some reason, I really liked this unassuming place.

Gazing absentmindedly back toward the tee box of the second hole, I noticed an older gentleman launch a ball with an ungraceful lurch before cautiously settling into a golf cart by himself. As he headed my way, my instinct was to flee toward the next hole in my own electric cart and avoid the inevitable small talk that results when golfers are randomly paired up. Whenever a stranger and I link up on a golf course, they either wear trucker hats that say "Support Day Drinking" and puff huge cigars, or they turn out to be the club champion for the past eleven years. Both scenarios are unsettling.

But something caused me to ignore my instinct to flee and, instead, I waited courteously for the white-haired man in the cart to hit his second shot. From where his drive had landed in the fairway, he hit a "worm burner" that bounced precariously close to my cart before caroming off a faded wooden sign that read "out of bounds" and disappearing into one of those shallow ponds created by Florida developers that harbor alligators.

I invited him to join me on the green and, as is the custom in golf everywhere, we vigorously apologized in advance for the sorry state of our games. Don had sparkling blue eyes and a pleasant, plump face that had begun to droop into jowls. It was just after Christmas, and the notion of "a jolly old elf" came to mind. He had a modest paunch and significant edema in both legs, which made him walk with a waddling gait that looked uncomfortable.

We teed off on the third hole and ventured forth together, the golf highly erratic, but the company easy and pleasant. For seven more holes on a mild, sun-splashed South Florida day, we settled into friendly chatter. Don was a Missouri native (he pronounced it *Missour-uh*) and had a diverse background in several branches of engineering. He had served in Korea, was happily married for many years, and spent winters in Florida since retirement. I was a primary care physician from Boston, closing in on retirement and enjoying my first taste of a winter free of ice and snow. We instinctively enjoyed one another's company and agreed to meet again at a slightly more upscale course the following week.

After that round (naturally, we were paired with a past club champion this time), we ate lunch in the clubhouse and delved deeper into who we really were, beyond the superficial banter of the golf course.

Besides his service in the Marine Corps and lengthy career as an engineer, Don was a student of the bible. He believed in the power of love and forgiveness with more certainty now in his eighties than at any time in his life. He told me about his family and asked with friendly curiosity about mine.

I acknowledged that my only son, Graham, had passed away at twenty-two from a seizure complicated by a cardiac arrest. I had written a book about him called *Jabberwocky*, which was on the verge of being published. Graham had been born with cerebral palsy, and the book was about the surprising epiphanies we experienced, along with his mom, at a magical place on the island of Martha's Vineyard called Camp Jabberwocky. I mentioned with pride that a celebrity endorsement from Katie Couric had referred to the book as "the story of a beautiful boy who showed us a life without limits and embodied the power of love." I had some early copies of the book in my car, and something told me to give one to Don as we parted ways in the parking lot.

We had planned to connect again soon to play golf, but Don called me the next day to say that he wasn't feeling well and was probably too weak to play anytime soon in the Florida heat.

"What about lunch instead?"

"Of course," I said, chuckling when he proposed that we meet at his favorite restaurant, Larry's Lunchbox.

"The best Reuben sandwiches in Florida," he promised.

A few days later, tucked among tax offices, nail salons, and consignment shops, I found Larry's in a typical Florida strip mall. Don was waiting, and a bubbly waitress sat us at a table on the narrow sidewalk outside, a concession to the COVID-19 pandemic. Don and I removed our masks and placed an order for two Reuben sandwiches with cream sodas. We looked at each other in silence for a few moments, and something seemed to pass between us, what Rabbi Lawrence Kushner might describe as an "invisible line of connection." I began to feel that there had been a reason that I had waited for Don on the second hole at Pelican Shores.

Apparently, he was feeling the same thing, and we regarded one another not as new acquaintances do, but as if we'd been friends for a long time. We talked for a while about the mess that the world was in over the roar of passing delivery trucks and the occasional revving of an Italian luxury car pulling into a parking spot in front of Larry's.

The waitress served our sandwiches, and we each took a bite, savoring the unique flavors of a perfect Reuben sandwich, just as Don had promised. As my new friend looked straight at me with those intense blue eyes, I returned his gaze and suddenly realized we were both beginning to cry. I sensed that something about the apparent hazard of our meeting had triggered in both of us an acute appreciation for lives that had been marked by gratitude and love.

But I went ahead and asked him anyway, "Don, why are we crying?"

"I read your book," he said.

TWO CORNED BEEF

Izzy Arbeiter's daughter, Fran, told me that his favorite lunch was corned beef on dark rye with a side of potato salad. I stopped at a popular deli named Barry's and bought two of the sandwiches along with two cans of Doctor Brown's cream soda and a tub of the potato salad.

Somehow, the bill came to thirty-three dollars. Apparently, that was the going rate in the Boston suburbs, but I paid it happily in the hope that it might bring some small pleasure to Izzy, who had landed in the hospital the day before.

At age ninety-six, Izzy had begun to lose his balance. That surprised me, because I had visited him six weeks earlier at his home and he seemed robust then, walking confidently around the well-kept colonial house that overlooked the Charles River, ten miles west of Boston. When he greeted me at the front door that day, his white hair was impeccably combed, his eyes sparkled, and he looked elegant in a navy-blue polo shirt under a tailored sport coat. We visited for a while with his wife Anna and exchanged updates about our families. Izzy's face lit up with pride when I helped him hang some framed photos of his children and grandchildren in the living room.

Eventually, my friend escorted me to the back porch where we sat quietly for a few minutes, watching dappled afternoon light sparkle on the river that flowed gently beyond his back lawn. Izzy then gathered himself and began the astonishing story of survival he had promised to share with me.

In January of 1945, with the Red Army approaching from the east, Adolph Hitler ordered the evacuation of the Nazi extermination camps. Not quite twenty years old, Izzy was among the skeletal survivors of Auschwitz, the infamous prison in southern Poland where over a million souls had perished. In that terrifying place, he had improbably survived for nearly four years.

On the morning of January 27, without warning in the frigid pre-dawn gloom, Nazi guards viciously herded Izzy and dozens of trembling men and women through the camp's main gate. Emerging beneath the infamous metal sign that read *Arbeit Macht Frei* (Work Sets You Free), the emaciated prisoners were ordered to begin a "death march" toward the interior of the German Reich. In an attempt to hide the scale of mass murder that took place at Auschwitz, the Nazis began destroying gas chambers, crematoria, and reams of documents. The death march was intended to prevent prisoners from being liberated by the Allies and testifying about the atrocities they had endured. Unfortunately for the Nazis, that strategy failed to account for the thousands of inmates near death from starvation and disease still inside the camp when the Red Army arrived.

As the Russians confronted the haunting scene of sick and dying prisoners, mass graves and macabre piles of shoes and eyeglasses, the death march continued. Days blurred together in the brutal cold, as Izzy and the other disoriented prisoners marched numbly ahead, moving deeper into Nazi-controlled territory. Periodically, the German guards apathetically shot stragglers, leaving them to bleed to death where they fell.

Moments of terror were all too familiar to Izzy and the others, but when the Nazi commander ordered them to sit down on the side of the road, they felt a primal rush of fear. Fully expecting death in a hail of machine gun fire, surreal moments followed as the prisoners watched the SS soldiers simply walk ahead without a word and disappear into the distance. Reality itself seemed to dissolve as the stunned men and women scrambled into the adjacent forest and hid. Unimaginably, the Nazis did not return.

Time passed in a strange, discontinuous way. Izzy was disoriented and close to death from starvation and exposure when a voice in his head told him to start moving. Emerging from the forest, he wandered aimlessly along a country road and stumbled into an old barn. For a few moments, he was sure that he was hallucinating. Directly in front of him, in one of the stalls, sat a Nazi motorcycle. More bizarre still, there was gas in the tank and a key in the ignition.

Izzy had never ridden a motorcycle. But he was too exhausted to walk any further and, after enduring years of unspeakable barbarity, what appeared before him was a deus ex machina—quite literally in his case—a machine from God. And a BMW at that. After being "bucked off" several times, Izzy managed to figure out the machine's clutch and rode away. In the dissociated fog of his brain, a bizarre question formed: Was it possible that he had survived the Holocaust?

When he was stopped (and nearly arrested!) at an American checkpoint, a soldier oriented him to where they were and told him that the Germans were in a desperate retreat from the Eastern Front. In disbelief, Izzy struggled to comprehend what had seemed impossible for so long: The horror of Nazi tyranny—the sadistic madness of the Holocaust—was ending.

The troops at the checkpoint gave Izzy food and gas for the BMW and helped him formulate a plan. There was a Jewish group at General Eisenhower's headquarters in Stuttgart, in the American Zone of Occupation, that was collecting information on survivors. Izzy desperately needed to know if any of his family members were alive. There was also the matter of a woman named Anna, whom he had met in the camps. Could she have survived? With only faint hope in his heart, Izzy set off for Stuttgart.

After a dreamlike journey on bombed-out roads, Izzy reached the Allied base. His arrival, on what he referred to as the "borrowed" Nazi motorcycle, produced astonishment among the soldiers at the base entrance, and he was brought to the attention of an American major. Startled by Izzy's cadaverous appearance, the man personally escorted him to a locker room for a shower—his first in over four years—and gave him clean clothing, food, and a cot. The camp uniform was burned.

Just one of his four brothers had survived. Izzy's parents and the youngest brother, seven-year-old Motek, had been murdered at Treblinka.

Anna was alive.

When I found his hospital room, Izzy looked markedly different. It had been less than two months since I had last seen him, but he was noticeably frail now and spoke in a whisper. Neither hip had been broken when he fell at home, and his heart was pumping adequately, but something irrevocable had happened, almost as if age itself had simply caught up to him. I began to realize that, before Izzy would reach the age of ninety-seven in a few months, the inexorable effects of time were going to end a life that Mengele, the Gestapo, and the SS were unable to extinguish.

I watched my friend contentedly sipping the chicken noodle soup the hospital had sent up on a tray with some Saltine crackers and tried to imagine him surviving for four years on watery, unappetizing rutabaga broth and scraps of bread. I was unable to fathom that or any of the other torments Izzy had endured. As he dozed off, I reflected on the shocking history that he had shared with me on my visit to his home.

Antisemitism was prevalent in Izzy's hometown of Płock in central Poland long before the Nazis arrived when he was fourteen. With the arrival of the Germans, however, the persecution of Jews was "radicalized." Rumors of a

"Final Solution to the Jewish Problem" were whispered at night among worried families. For the next two years, Izzy was forced to work as a "slave" to a Gestapo officer who beat him for failing to perfectly polish his hobnailed Jackboots—an apt symbol of the totalitarianism that was coming.

The Arbeiter home was seized, and Izzy, his parents, and four brothers were forced into a newly created ghetto in the central district of Warsaw. A ten-foot-high wall topped with barbed wire eventually held over 400,000 Jews there under armed guard.

Around the time Izzy turned sixteen, the Nazis' brutal behavior escalated into unabashed sadism, and the family faced a scene of abject horror. SS officers with frothing dogs forced families from the ghetto into a small square and announced what they called a "selection." In a frenzy of confusion and terror, people deemed unable to work—the very old and very young—were herded to the left side of the square. Those judged able to work were driven to the right side. As children screamed, Izzy's parents and seven-year-old brother were pushed to the left while the four older Arbeiter boys were forced at gunpoint to the right.

In the turmoil, Izzy failed to understand what was happening, and he ran to the left, where his parents and youngest brother clung together. His father grabbed his collar and pushed him back across the square after making him swear that—if he survived what was to come—he would carry on the family's traditions and their Jewish faith. That afternoon, the Arbeiter parents and little Motek were loaded onto a cattle car bound for Treblinka. The older brothers were shipped to three different "labor camps." Izzy was ultimately destined for the death camp called Auschwitz.

A nurse entered the room to draw blood, but somehow Izzy remained half asleep during the procedure. Watching him, my thoughts turned to the contrasts in our lives. At an age when I mowed a few lawns in a quiet Boston suburb and bought baseball cards with my profits, Izzy was assigned to peel the charred bodies of prisoners off the high-voltage wires of Auschwitz, where they had hurled themselves, preferring suicide to relentless savagery. At the age when I was self-consciously flirting with girls in the cafeteria at my college, Izzy served as a *scheissmeister*, collecting human feces from the Auschwitz latrines with a shovel, loading the unspeakable waste into a wagon, and dumping it into a putrid pond near the border of the camp for use in the spring as fertilizer. At times, on return trips from the pond, he smuggled bread in the wagon from a kindly farmer whose property neighbored the camp, concealing the food in buckets soiled with feces and urine.

When Izzy finished his nap, I took out the sandwiches and potato salad and asked him to clarify for me how he had found the woman who became his sweetheart and, ultimately, his wife. From our earlier conversation, I was aware that they had been lovestruck from a distance in the madness of Auschwitz.

Izzy's eyes lit up, and he told me an amusing story about riding the BMW from Stuttgart to a DPC (Displaced Persons Camp) in Germany, where Anna was living in a single room with five young women who shared a single pair of shoes. Ignoring the passionate warnings of her roommates, Anna agreed to come away with Izzy. Three months later, they were married, initiating a union of seventy-five years that ultimately produced three children, four grandchildren, and three great-grandchildren.

A year later, Izzy and Anna excitedly said goodbye to the DPC where they were living and boarded a ship bound for Boston, where Izzy's aunt served as their sponsor. As such, she promised the American government that she would find housing and assistance for her nephew and his wife until they became self-sufficient. Uncle Sam expected sponsors to keep their loved ones off the welfare rolls.

Izzy, of course, had no intention of becoming a public "charge" and, soon after arriving in New England, he started a successful laundry and dry-cleaning business. His impish humor was evident when I asked him to tell me more about that venture.

"I was a CPA," said Izzy. After I raised my eyebrows, he mischievously added, "Cleaning, pressing, and alterations!"

Izzy was not one to talk about himself, but I knew that he had become a community leader after settling in the Boston suburb of Auburndale. He was a co-founder of the New England Holocaust Memorial and a sought-after speaker in Massachusetts schools and at conferences in Europe, telling and retelling the story of the Holocaust.

Watching Izzy nibbling at the big sandwich, a bizarre question entered my mind. It was so macabre that I wondered if I should refrain from even articulating it to my friend. But a trust had grown between us, and I went ahead.

"Izzy, I'm sitting here trying to imagine you in the camp, surviving for so long on fragments of bread and watery soup. Some eighty years later, here we are, sharing two huge corned beef sandwiches and potato salad as if such a meal is quite normal. My God, Izzy—did you ever dream of someone bringing a meal like this to you at Auschwitz?"

"Before you took ten steps inside the gate, you would have been killed for that sandwich," he replied.

I then asked Izzy if he had any idea why he had survived when six million others, including most of his family, had perished. Was it chance, or was it something else? I had asked him the same question before, but now, as he apparently neared death, I asked him again.

He whispered that he had wondered about that for nearly eight decades, discussed it with rabbis, scholars, and theologians, but he had never been able to find an explanation.

"There is no answer," he said.

Postscript:

A few weeks later, Israel Arbeiter passed away. At his memorial service, Izzy was remembered for his astonishing resilience, dedication to family, and service to the Jewish community. He was honored for his testimony at the Nuremberg Trials and at Days of Remembrance in Europe by a representative of the German government. His decades of teaching scholars and ordinary people about the *Shoah* were applauded. But it was Izzy's children who poignantly commemorated the proudest achievement of his life: he had kept the promise that he made to his father in the square outside Warsaw eighty years earlier.

Surviving unspeakable cruelty, he had lived and kept alive his family's traditions and their Jewish faith, a heritage that thrives today in multiple generations of the Arbeiter family in America.

ORPHANAGE FOUR

During the summer when I was introduced to Kim Schecter, I was working on a photography project at Massachusetts General Hospital that consisted of portraits of unusually resilient people. Many were patients facing existential challenges, including cancer, and, despite frightening adversity, their expressions often revealed dignity and courage.

At the time, I was corresponding with my young friend and de facto goddaughter, Julia Grace, an aspiring poet at Bates College in Lewiston, Maine. When she moved down to the Boston area after graduation, "Jules" and I came up with an idea for a project that would allow us to spend some time together and expose us to inspiring people we might not otherwise meet. With luck, we might interview and photograph individuals in the community who had faced extraordinary challenges and responded to them with strength and uncommon grace. Through a contact at MGH, Jules and I met a gentleman named Alex Schecter, a business leader active in the Jewish community around Boston. When we explained the project to Alex, he said, "You should definitely meet my father!"

Two weeks later, eighty-five-year-old Kim Schecter and his wife, Lena, warmly greeted Jules and me at their home in the Boston suburb of Watertown. The sunny second-floor apartment in a cluster of brick buildings was filled with family photos, mementos, and the welcoming scent of baking bread. Kim looked a decade younger than his age in a plaid shirt, faded jeans, and tennis shoes. He had a rugged build, was a bit bow-legged, and sported a salt and pepper goatee. I noticed a tennis racket in a corner and asked him if he still played.

"Of course I do!" he said. "Let's hit some balls if the rain stops."

Jules and I explained our project and visited for a while with Kim, Lena, and their daughter, Masha, who translated for us from Russian, the Schecters' preferred language. Jules and I were immediately touched by the unusual warmth and graciousness extended to us by the family. Lena served cookies and tea, and we gathered around a comfortable kitchen table.

"Mr. Schecter, your son, Alex, tells us that you might have quite a story to share," I started.

"Indeed, he does!" offered Masha.

Kim was pensive for a few moments and closed his eyes. As he prepared to begin the story of his childhood, his emotions rose. Dabbing his eyes with a handkerchief and blinking back tears, he struggled to compose himself. Jules and I shared the realization that the poignancy of Kim's early memories was viscerally transporting him some eighty years into the past.

From a shelf in the adjacent sitting room, Lena produced faded sepia images of Kim's parents and carefully set them down on the paisley tablecloth on the kitchen table. His father, Miron, was a handsome, robust-looking man who had managed a local dairy in Dunaevtsy (*doo-nah-EETS-y*), their small village in Ukraine, where Kim was born in 1935. Kim's mother, Esfir, a diminutive and pretty young woman, was a homemaker and dressmaker. Their community in the southwestern part of Ukraine was then part of the Soviet Union.

Kim composed himself and began by describing his carefree days as a young boy, playing with the kids in his neighborhood and attending kindergarten. When school let out in the afternoon, he loved to drop in on his grandmother, who invariably passed him his favorite culinary treat through a kitchen window: freshly baked bread dipped in olive oil and sugar. For the rest of his life, in fact,

Kim would crave the comforting aroma and earthy taste of bread, especially when it was still warm from the oven.

At home in Dunaevtsy, Kim spoke Yiddish. At kindergarten, he spoke Ukrainian. Like kids everywhere, he relished the freedom and happy-go-lucky days of childhood.

But, as World War II expanded eastward, the tranquility of Kim's small village was fractured. Jewish families like the Schecter's began to realize that what had once seemed unthinkable had become reality: Hitler's plan to occupy Central Europe and the Soviet Union, enslave entire communities—and exterminate them—was actually happening. The Schecters' village was in the direct path of the Nazi horror that was rapidly advancing from Poland into Ukraine.

Miron knew that he might be conscripted into the Red Army of Russia at any time. Recognizing the imminent danger to his family, he made the momentous decision to move Kim and Esfir, then eight months pregnant, to the city of Fergana, Uzbekistan, one thousand miles away, skirting the southern border of Russia and the Caspian Sea. He wanted his wife and son as far away as possible from the German advance. The timing of Miron's decision was providential. Only a week after fleeing with his family, the nightmare of Nazism reached Dunaevtsy. Mass killings of Jews, including Kim's grandparents and other relatives, took place in the village square. Men, women, and children were lined up on the edge of newly dug pits and impassively shot in the head, their bodies falling into macabre piles.

Probably unaware of how narrowly they had escaped the Nazi massacre at home, Miron, Esfir, and Kim continued the desperate trek to Fergana, an odyssey that took two arduous months on overloaded trains, horse-drawn carts, and—for long stretches—on foot. Kim remembers bombs exploding as they crossed a river and seeing massive fields of wheat on fire.

During the journey, Esfir's pregnancy became progressively difficult with what may have been preeclampsia, and she was admitted to a maternity hospital when they finally arrived in Uzbekistan. Shortly after giving birth, she died of sepsis, and, unthinkably, her newborn son also died just a few days later.

At some point, Miron was ordered to report for active duty by the Red Army. He made the decision to leave Kim in Fergana, in the care of two women the family had known back in Ukraine. Fergana was an industrial city surrounded by mountains, with an eclectic population that included Russians, Uzbeks, and Tatars. The two women agreed to care for the boy in a small home on the edge of the city. But, shortly after Miron departed for his military duty, something in their circumstances changed dramatically. Instead of keeping Kim at home, the women abruptly admitted him to an orphanage. They had no way to communicate this change of plans or the reason for it to Kim's father.

In the grim place that Kim would call home for the next five years, a thousand orphaned children resided in overcrowded barracks. Barely six years old, Kim suddenly faced the prospect of surviving by himself in a foreign land where he could not understand a single word of the language. In his new "dormitory," one of dozens in what was known as *Orphanage Four*, he shared a single bed with another youngster who lay at night in the opposite direction. There were eighteen of those narrow beds crammed into each room.

While the mood in Fergana, like much of eastern Europe and central Asia at the time, was tense and uncertain, Kim was treated humanely in his new home. The organizers of the orphanages, along with the ordinary citizens of Uzbekistan, accepted a total of nearly 200,000 lost children during the course of World War II, reminding the world that compassion still existed at a time when the evil of Nazism was spreading. Despite the kindness of the Uzbeks, however, there were simply not enough staff to properly supervise the children in the orphanages or to offer much in the way of formal schooling for youngsters like Kim. Most of the time, he was simply on his own, a forlorn child facing an uncertain future in an unfamiliar land.

Elsewhere in Europe, unlike in Uzbekistan, there were terrible instances of neglect and abuse of orphans. Known as "wolf children," some boys and girls ended up living by their wits in the forests of Lithuania or begging on bombed-out city streets. Roaming the debris left of Europe, those children suffered from starvation, a plethora of physical illnesses, and unimaginable emotional trauma.

The children in Orphanage Four in Fergana were fortunate by comparison, but food was scarce. Stunting of the children's growth was common due to a lack of dietary protein. Kim ate vegetable soup each day, but none of the bread he loved, unless he or another kid could steal a loaf from a local market. There was essentially no animal protein in the children's diet, and most of them developed a form of malnutrition characterized by pale skin, bloating, and muscle wasting.

Not far from the orphanage, there were orchards owned by local families where ripe apples, pears, and peaches tantalizingly adorned the trees. Kim and a handful of other boys snuck out periodically to steal the fruit. After stuffing their haul into oversized shirts and pants, they would return to the orphanage and distribute the fruit to the younger children. On some of the forays into the orchards, Kim was chased by angry farmers. He was a nimble youngster, but, due to his malnutrition, he was "swollen all over" with edema and not as elusive as he would have normally been. By leaping over fences and running as hard as he could, he closely avoided capture several times. On those occasions, Kim was convinced that the furious farmer on his heels would cut his throat if he stumbled.

For five long years, Kim's mind continuously pictured his father, and he never gave up the hope that he and Miron would be reunited. Night after night, in vivid dreams, his father returned for him. By day, in a child's halting script, Kim wrote letters to the leaders of Uzbekistan and Russia, including the military figures Voroshilov and Molotov, asking for information about his father and urging them, *Please ask him to come for me.*

Periodically, Kim's hopelessness would overwhelm him, and he would run away from the orphanage, hoping that, by a miracle, he would find Miron. On a few occasions, he even jumped on trains, not knowing where they were going. When he was caught by the police on those outings, he wasn't completely devastated, because the officers typically gave him food before returning him to the orphanage. In the shared twin bed, he prayed at night, pleading with God to reunite him with his father, and he grieved continuously for his mother and little brother. His unwavering belief that he would see Miron again sustained him amid the bleakness of Orphanage Four.

When I interrupted Kim's chronicle and asked him about his remarkable faith, Masha translated his response: "I could *feel* that my father was alive. I could *feel* it."

On an overcast fall day, some five years after arriving at Orphanage Four, Kim snuck into one of the orchards with a group of boys to steal apples. Upon returning to the dorm, he heard his name called and was told to report immediately to the administrator's office. Having just clambered over several fences, his clothes were disheveled, and fruit juice was dripping down his shirt and trousers. Sure that he was in trouble for stealing, he prepared himself for punishment.

Trembling, he entered the office of the director, a kindly woman named Lyubov Ivanova. He noticed a soldier standing near her. The wiry man wore a grey uniform with dark epaulets. Two ribbons and a medal hung over his left chest. His hair was thinning at the temples.

The afternoon light was fading in Watertown, the rain had let up, and Kim looked as if he could use a break from the story. He and I headed out to the tennis court behind the apartment complex to hit some balls before it got dark. He had a powerful serve and moved well for a man his age. When it became too dark to see the balls any longer, we returned to the apartment.

In the kitchen, Lena opened a tin of pickled fish as a special tribute to Jules and me, the family's honored guests that day. Neither of us was necessarily a devotee of that sort of indulgence, but we appreciated the gesture and took some bites, as our host resumed his story.

At first, Kim did not recognize the soldier standing near the orphanage director. But a photograph sitting on her desk caught his attention. It was a picture of a small family. Improbably, it dawned on Kim that he had seen the photo before. It had been taken six or seven years ago in his village in Ukraine. In fact, it had hung on the wall of his family's living room. The people in the photo were Esfir, Miron, and Kim.

From the frayed photo, Kim's gaze turned to the man in uniform. Slowly at first, he began to grasp the possibility that the soldier standing before him might be the man in the photo. He had changed since Kim last saw him five years ago, but—incredibly—it dawned on Kim that the man in the photo was, indeed, the person standing right in front of him. The man was his father.

Miron recognized his son, ran to Kim, and wrapped him in a bear hug.

Father and son shared a long, poignant embrace. This was the deliverance Kim had never stopped believing would happen. This was the moment he had dreamed of during the nearly two thousand nights since his father left Fergana. This was the miracle Kim had prayed for night after night in the darkness of his dormitory room in Orphanage Four.

The administrator, Ms. Ivanova, then explained to Miron that there was paperwork to be completed in cases like this, and it would take a few days before she could release his son from Orphanage Four. Kim's father's reply was definitive:

"Actually, no, Director Ivanova! Thank you for taking care of my son for so long, and I am very grateful. But I will be taking my son right now, thank you very much. I hope it won't be necessary, but, if so, I would be happy to tell you what you can do with the paperwork!"

Jules and I allowed Kim a minute or two to compose himself after telling his incredible story. We drank hot tea with lemon, served by Lena, and chatted for a little while before asking him to fill in the background that led to the jubilant reunion with his father.

When the war ended, Miron was discharged from the army and traveled from Russia by train to look for his son in Uzbekistan. He went to hospitals and town halls in Tashkent and Fergana, asking for lists of orphans and their whereabouts. At first, he had no luck because, reminiscent of what happened so often at Ellis Island in New York Harbor, a harried Uzbek clerk had inadvertently changed Kim's name from the Hebrew *Kiva* to *Kim*. After a number of frustrating trips to government offices, Miron was told by a secretary in an administration building that there might be a Schecter boy with the first initial K at Orphanage Four in Fergana.

After the emotional reunion with Kim, Miron took his son to Gorky, Russia, where the family had some relatives and a few friends. Kim attended school there and developed a trade repairing clocks before being conscripted into the

Russian army at age eighteen. He was shipped to areas of anti-communist unrest and eventually served in Hungary and Poland.

He subsequently fell in love with Lena in Gorky, and their daughter Masha was born there in 1959. He continued to ply his trade as a clock repairman, sometimes completing jobs without charging his customers when he sensed that they were lacking in funds. Over the years, Kim became an accomplished tennis player and won several national tournaments in Russia. A son, Alex, was born there a decade later.

Eventually, Masha became an American citizen, followed by Alex, and, after a period of time living in Israel, Kim and Lena were ultimately able to follow Alex to the United States. Taking advantage of his skills in tennis, Kim spent much of his time in retirement teaching the game to youngsters in the Boston area. He also continued repairing clocks and watches.

Of note, part of the reason the Schecter family left Russia in 1990 was antisemitism. After all the family had endured during World War II, including the murder of loved ones by the Nazis, they sometimes found notes placed on the door of their home in Gorky, saying, "Jews go away!" An ugly reminder that the end of the Holocaust was by no means the end of antisemitism.

Kim and Lena allowed me to photograph them in their home before Jules and I departed. Looking at the images of their faces that night, I saw courage, resilience, and kindness.

After a long interval of not seeing the Schecter family, partly due to the pandemic, I made arrangements to visit them on a sunny fall day. I brought a copy of my book *Jabberwocky: Lessons of Love from a Boy Who Never Spoke* as a gift for previously sharing their time so generously and showing two strangers, Jules and me, such warmth. Masha was already familiar with the book and, in Russian, briefly summarized the story about Camp Jabberwocky and my son to Kim and Lena, mentioning that Graham had passed away at age twenty-two. Sitting directly across from me at the familiar kitchen table, I watched Kim carefully grasp the book in his rough hands and study the ethereal image of Graham's face on the cover, almost as if he was cradling it. Suddenly, he began to weep.

A potent wave of emotion passed among the four of us. What was it in that beautiful cover image that moved Kim so powerfully? In the photo, Graham was close to the age Kim was in those terrifying early days at the orphanage in Fergana. Did Kim see something in my son's face that recalled the powerful yearning he had experienced to be reconnected with his father, never giving up on the dream of recapturing a family in a world of incomprehensible turmoil? Or could he have seen in Graham's face, an impressionistic vision of the younger brother he would never know, Esfir's baby who perished at the end of the journey to Fergana? Or was that intense emotion something else entirely?

As I watched Kim's touching response to holding *Jabberwocky*, my own emotions rose, and I began to tear up. I suddenly felt an intense connection with this man who had shared his astonishing story of survival and faith with Jules and me. I wondered if it was *I* who was yearning for something. If so, what was I yearning for? Was it as simple as yearning to see Graham again one day when my turn comes to "cross over?" Or did Kim's story trigger a yearning for a connection with my own father, whom I had seen only rarely after my parents divorced when I was five years old, about the same age as Kim upon his arrival at the orphanage in Fergana?

I never really knew my father, a wonderful man who was haunted by alcoholism and PTSD throughout his life. Was there something in Kim's overwhelming yearning for Miron that I related to subliminally? Something I had long ago dismissed—a longing for a transcendent relationship with a father who would miraculously emerge into my life and remain part of it?

Whatever it was that moved us both to tears left an unmistakable feeling that Kim and I now shared an "invisible line of connection," to borrow the iconic phrase of Rabbi Lawrence Kushner. That potent sense was clear to both of us as we shared an embrace before I departed the Schecter home.

Just before the door closed, I glanced at Kim's tennis racket in the corner of the foyer, and we promised to hit some balls again. When that day comes, I am hopeful that we will sit down together alongside the court and discover more about the invisible line that connects us.

HOPE FOR TWO PEOPLE

"The quality of mercy is not strained;
It droppeth as the gentle rain from heaven
Upon the place beneath. It is twice blest;
It blesseth him that gives and him that takes."
—William Shakespeare,
The Merchant of Venice

It seems odd that I can't remember her name. When you quite literally save someone's life, shouldn't you remember their name? Or, possibly, I never actually knew her name. One of the nurses must have shared it with me, but I was probably too tired that night to remember names. I had been part of the humanitarian relief effort in Haiti for about three months then, after the massive 7.0 earthquake in January of 2010. I was stationed at L'Hôpital Albert Schweitzer in the village of Deschapelles, where cholera had broken out on the island's northern peninsula, in the valley of the Artibonite River. In that tiny hospital built in 1956 by Larry Mellon, a scion of the Mellon banking family of Pittsburgh, and his wife, Gwen, our small team of doctors and nurses faced an unrelenting influx of critically ill patients.

In over thirty years as a physician working primarily in Boston, I had seen a wide spectrum of human afflictions, but I had never witnessed anything like the cholera epidemic that was rapidly spreading across Haiti. At the hospital in Deschapelles, scores of villagers near death arrived faster than our nurses could triage them, appearing on the rusted beds of mud-caked pickup trucks, on the backs of donkeys, and even carried like sacks of sugar cane on the shoulders of family members. Our makeshift cholera team consisted of a few doctors from Haiti, along with volunteer physicians and nurses from the United States, Switzerland, and Poland.

When every bed in the hospital was filled, we were forced to treat the incoming patients on army cots in the sweltering heat of the outdoor foyer of the main building. Sheltered by a few bushy mango trees on a battered wall near the entrance was a crude plaque that celebrated Dr. Schweitzer's ethos: *Respe Pou Lavi* (Reverence for Life).

As an internist at Massachusetts General Hospital in Boston, I had volunteered to be a member of the hospital's Global Disaster Response Team. Haiti was my first "deployment" in this role, and more than one veteran of the team warned me that it would be a shocking initiation.

Our MGH group worked under the auspices of several large international humanitarian organizations, including Project Hope. These NGOs (non-government organizations) recruit medical professionals from around the world and interact with dozens of other teams, like Doctors Without Borders, when natural disasters or wars create public health emergencies around the globe. I had studied epidemiology as a graduate student at the Harvard School of Public Health three decades earlier, but it was abundantly clear that no amount of classroom learning could have prepared me for practicing medicine in the chaotic aftermath of an actual disaster. I had no idea if my set of medical skills would even be of use in a place like Haiti. But my colleagues at MGH were willing to cover me for three months and encouraged me to go.

When the cholera outbreak occurred, I had already spent several weeks in the refugee camps in the teeming capital city of Port-au-Prince, where the damage from the earthquake was catastrophic. The squalor in those camps (one had sprouted on the foul surface of a toxic waste dump) had hardened me and tempered my naive hope that well-meaning foreign volunteers could make a dent in the misery of Haiti. In Port-au-Prince, I had wondered if I had stumbled into a hellhole that was truly without hope, a place abandoned by God and man.

When communicating with colleagues at home, I found it impossible to describe Haiti in words. Understanding Haiti was visceral. You needed to smell the stench of festering garbage and overflowing latrines. You needed to walk past crumpled buildings that encased corpses. You needed to hear the brutal throbbing of Creole rap music blasting from dilapidated taxis. You needed to breathe the fetid dust that covered the dirt roads and eroded hills. You needed to see emaciated patients with AIDS and TB sleeping on benches in shanty towns made up of rusting tin huts.

But you also needed to listen to the laughter of the children of Haiti. Surrounded by wretchedness that even the poorest children in the US will never experience, their innocent howls of joy and delight were uplifting. Like the vibrant red blossoms on bougainvillea bushes that sprouted from the country's ravaged surface, the laughter of the children was a promise that Haiti would survive, as it had through so many other disasters inflicted upon it by man and nature.

In the scheme of life-threatening diseases, cholera is relatively easy to treat. The cholera bacteria are ingested in contaminated water, resulting in relentless diarrhea and vomiting. The disease typically clears in a few days, even without antibiotics, provided an adequate amount of the lost fluid is replaced. Gatorade, or any beverage containing sugar and salt, works well in early cases, provided the patient is well enough to drink. Those who receive fluid rapidly enough, by mouth or intravenously, generally survive. But if they live far away or if they wait too long to come in, they can die of "circulatory collapse." Simply put, they no longer have enough fluid in their bloodstream to maintain the blood pressure that is needed to bring oxygen to the body's vital organs.

Some residents of the Artibonite Valley held voodoo beliefs. One was that an illness like cholera was the result of a curse, not an infectious disease. As the epidemic spread around Deschapelles, herbal remedies and "faith healing" were offered to the villagers by *houngans* (priests) or *manbos* (priestesses). Some people sickened by cholera were embarrassed to seek help from "Western medicine" until it was too late.

When I arrived at L'Hôpital Albert Schweitzer, I had never seen a case of cholera, let alone managed a growing outbreak of a virulent disease. Shortly after my arrival, I was joined by an unassuming senior pediatrician from Switzerland. To our mutual amazement, we found ourselves essentially in charge. Two American doctors who were at the hospital when we arrived were burned out and long gone within twenty-four hours. The challenge facing my Swiss colleague and me was not only treating the sick but devising strategies to prevent the spread of the disease to everyone else around the hospital campus. Three earnest young interns showed up from Poland, eager to help, along with a group of benevolent volunteer nurses from the US. We did the best we could to cope with a relentless influx of very sick people. In the country as a whole, there would be more than 800,000 Haitians sickened by cholera and 10,000 deaths before the epidemic was over.

Our team quickly learned to look for simple clues that cholera patients were becoming dangerously dehydrated. They were in trouble if their eyes appeared sunken, their pulses were weak, or their skin had lost its elasticity. At that stage of the disease, cholera was a medical emergency. One of us needed to find a way to get fluid back into the patient's bloodstream or bone marrow quickly, or they would die.

When I was transferred from Port-au-Prince to help with the cholera outbreak in Deschapelles, there was about a month left in the commitment I had made to MGH and the relief agencies. Port-au-Prince had been deemed too dangerous for us due to kidnappings, and, by that time, every instinct in my body was telling me to just go home. Get back to a place of safety, clean water, and freedom from despair. What possible difference was my presence in Haiti making, anyway? In the end, I resolved to stay, having been taught from childhood to honor commitments. Working up to twenty hours a day under harsh conditions, I wasn't sure I could make it. I found a calendar and began to check off the days until I could leave Deschapelles with my honor and self-esteem intact.

After three weeks of battling cholera around the clock, I neared exhaustion. I saw no humor in my dormitory circumstances: six roommates in a tiny hospital room who snored like cartoon ducks. I found a huge industrial fan one night and turned it on next to the loudest of them. My life was reduced to a numb, mechanical cycle: sleep for a few hours, put on scrubs, count the new patients, try to start IVs, ration the few remaining antibiotics, eat some beans and rice, give heartbreaking news to another family, try to sleep again. I was suffering burnout and knew it, too depleted physically, mentally, and emotionally to feel much empathy for my patients or their families. I just wanted to go home.

During supper, just a couple of days before I was scheduled to leave, one of the three zealous Polish interns, a brainy, bespeckled, young man named Jarek, burst breathlessly into our little dining area and asked if I would go back to the clinic with him to help resuscitate a woman in dire distress. Neither he nor the very capable Haitian and American nurses had been able to get an IV line into her collapsed veins. Her blood pressure was dropping, and she was about to die.

Together, we pushed our way through the familiar horde of beggars that perpetually loitered around our quarters and sprinted across the one hundred yards or so of gravel that separated our dining area from the clinic building. Rushing into the bleak concrete ward that reeked of body fluids, I saw Jarek's patient at the end of a line of cots. She looked about forty years old. She was surrounded by family members who were weeping and chanting in Creole. I knelt at her right side on the rough concrete floor and felt for a pulse. Nothing. I put my ear close to her mouth, listening for even a faint breath. Nothing. She was pulseless and not breathing. In a word, she was dead.

The family gazed at me with desperate hope. The nurses, too, stared at me, their expressions fervently challenging me to do *something*. Jarek and his fellow Polish intern, Luka, scrutinized me, hoping to follow a heroic order that might change the inevitable outcome.

Kneeling on the foul floor in my dirty green scrubs, I felt all those eyes on me. Nothing in my training had prepared me for a moment like this. I was a primary care internist, not a trauma surgeon, not a doctor trained in emergency procedures. But the pleading eyes remained fixed on mine, and I realized that I had to do something, even if it was essentially a sham. I needed to show the family, the nurses, and the interns that no heroic measure, no last resort, no matter how sure to fail, had been neglected.

I asked Jarek for a large-bore IV needle and catheter. To gain access to the patient's bloodstream, I decided to attempt a "femoral stick," placing a plastic catheter through a puncture in the groin, allowing access to the large vein that drains blood from the leg. I had never done this myself and had only seen it once or twice, thirty-five years earlier, during my residency training in the emergency room at MGH. Even there, in far more experienced hands, I recalled that the attempt was almost invariably unsuccessful.

The procedure is done by entering the skin with a large needle a centimeter or so inside the pulse from the femoral artery, which courses through the groin on its path to the leg. Once the needle is positioned in the vein, a catheter is then threaded into the vessel by carefully sliding it around the needle. The woman on the cot, however, had no femoral pulse at all to serve as a landmark for me, and there was no realistic possibility that the procedure could work. But at least I could look at the family and say we had tried everything. The weeping and chanting continued as I pushed the large needle blindly into the place in the patient's groin where I hoped the femoral vein might be.

To my astonishment, vigorous blood flowed back into the catheter around the needle, indicating that the IV line was successfully positioned in the patient's right femoral vein. Daring not to move even a millimeter despite pain in my knees from the concrete floor, I directed Luka to attach a liter bag of IV fluid via a tube into the catheter I was pinching precariously between my right thumb and index finger. I watched in awe as the saline solution passed easily into the catheterized vein. I ordered Luka to run the fluid "wide open," allowing the full liter to empty into the patient's circulation in about a minute.

And yet our patient did not breathe. She had no discernible heartbeat. Without daring to move from my frozen position, I told Luka to attach a second liter of saline and push it into the tube even faster, literally squeezing the bag with his hands. And the same with a third liter. Still, there was no response from the patient. We were simply too late. As Luka attached a fourth bag of saline to the IV tubing, I looked up dejectedly at the head of the cot, preparing to announce to the family that we were stopping.

At that exact moment, the patient opened her eyes.

She looked wildly around the cot with a startled expression. She coughed. She was breathing. A nurse announced that there was a pulse in her left arm. I knelt on the floor for another two or three minutes as Luka continued to manage the bags of IV saline, finally slowing the infusion down to a slow drip. We taped my IV carefully in place in the patient's groin, and I stood up for the first time in six or seven minutes, my shins scraped and my knees stiff and aching. Tears of joy were flowing all around the cot, while I tried hard to hide the fact that I was the most stunned person in the room. The patient's family probably thought that this femoral vein magic trick was something I performed routinely.

As I walked back to the dining area a few minutes later, I barely felt my feet touching the ground. Making my way through the pack of beggars, I wasn't sure if I should shout, sing, or cry. I had just done something that I didn't know how to do, something that had absolutely no chance of working.

What in the world had just happened?

I saw our patient outside the clinic the next morning, waiting for her son, a middle school principal, to take her home. She was radiant and beautiful. In fact, I was not sure I had ever seen anyone who looked healthier. Her son thanked me and took a picture of the two of us on a bench outside the hospital. Goodbyes were said, and we exchanged contact information. Unfortunately, the slip of paper her son handed me was misplaced as we turned our attention to the relentless stream of new patients arriving at the hospital on that beautiful Caribbean morning.

The next day, I took a final walk around the hospital campus and took some photos as mementos. Children were playing behind the clinic building, where families hung the laundry of loved ones who were inpatients in the hospital. In that unremarkable area, beneath makeshift clothes lines, I spotted a small bronze plaque that I hadn't noticed before:

> *"You are not able to change the world, but you are able to give hope to one human being."*
>
> *—Albert Schweitzer*

Two nights later, I left Deschapelles. A guarded minibus picked me up at 4:00 AM. (Traveling by day was dangerous due to robberies and kidnappings on the roads to Port-au-Prince.) I left my clothes and toiletries with the beggars, along with a few dollars and an old iPod. In the grimy van that took me to the airport on rutted dirt roads, I felt intense emotions. Selfishly, I experienced an overwhelming relief that I was finally going home and a nearly euphoric sense of deliverance from the relentless squalor that had haunted my every waking moment for the past three months.

As we neared the airport, the first weak orange rays of dawn appeared, and through the stained windows of the van, I began to discern shadows beside the road. I looked more closely and realized that the shapes were, in fact, human beings. Scores of people, still homeless three months after the earthquake, were sleeping out in the open on the narrow island between the road and the barbed wire fence around the airport.

Despite the efforts of our MGH team and the dozens of other relief organizations that had come to Haiti with skill and kindness, the suffering of those shadowy souls suddenly seemed inexorable, as if misery was simply their fate.

During a long wait in the airport, I fell asleep. In one dream, my own son was a hungry Haitian boy lurking in an alleyway. In another, I clearly saw the vibrant face of the woman we had saved, whose name escaped me. The boarding announcement woke me up, and I wondered for a moment where I was. I found an aisle seat and struggled to understand the meaning of what had happened two nights earlier in the valley of the Artibonite River.

In those surreal moments on the plane, an aphorism came to me in a half-dream. It was a passage from the Talmud: "*Whosoever saves even one human life saves all mankind.*"

Through a fog of weariness, I suddenly felt a profound sense of gratitude. I was grateful that I had chosen a career in medicine, grateful that I was part of an extraordinary institution like MGH, and proud that I had volunteered to go to Haiti. The warnings I had received three months earlier had been spot on. It had, indeed, been a shocking introduction to global health.

As my flight prepared to land in Boston and I soaked in the city's familiar skyline, my heart was full. I had honored my commitment. I was home. I was safe. And I was poised to resume *normalcy* in a place free from hunger, violence, and fear. But, for a while, my thoughts remained in Haiti, and I wondered about the radiant woman with cholera whose name still escaped me.

And even now, long after settling into the familiar rhythms of my life at home, I continue to wonder about her. I am not yet sure that I understand what happened that night in the cholera ward at L'Hôpital Albert Schweitzer in the valley of the Artibonite River in Haiti's Northern Peninsula. Placing a catheter into her right femoral vein was surely pure luck.

Wasn't it?

Dear Bud,

I am no longer the man I was before. During the time we lived and traveled together, something happened to me. Something I will think about with gratitude for the rest of my life.

All my love,
Dad

A BIT OF COMEDIC RELIEF

Disclaimer:

With apologies to those mentioned in the following pages, especially certain family members, I hope these anecdotes will bring a smile or, even better, a laugh loud enough to annoy the neighbors. Please proceed with caution.

DOCTOR STEVE HAS FUN WITH TECHNOLOGY

These thoughts are dedicated to those of you who, like me, have never figured out whether or not to accept cookies.

I hadn't been on vacation for a long time and couldn't wait to get to Colorado to go hiking with some friends from college. It was the time of year when the aspen leaves turn gloriously gold, and I looked forward to recharging my batteries in the Rocky Mountain air above the quaint village of Beaver Creek.

For some reason, when I reached the Hertz counter at the Eagle Airport, the only vehicle left was a Ford Explorer the size of a small school bus. It was about midnight, and I was very tired and stressed after being squeezed in a middle seat for six hours between a giant bearded man holding a box containing a meowing cat and a morbidly obese woman whose panniculus leaked over the armrest onto my lap when she doubled over to clean toe jam from her feet. When I attempted to direct a jet of air at her toes from the overhead vents (known in the airline industry as "gaspers"), the pulverized jam became aerosolized, sending trillions of minute flecks of the material into the far reaches of the cabin, where they could be inhaled by all on board.

So, I was happy to finally have some personal space, and there was plenty of it in the Special Edition Explorer, which had three rows of seats, a massive storage area, and steered like a dump truck. I set off on the interstate to Vail, hoping not to fall asleep and kill myself along with the dozens of long-haul truckers who were passing me on both sides at eighty-five miles per hour in thundering big rigs. When I flicked on the turn signal to change lanes, the rear window wiper began furiously oscillating, although it wasn't raining. In the dark, I considered the nearly infinite number of ways to turn, flick, push, pull, press, squeeze, and otherwise manipulate the blinker switch (that apparently had dozens of other purposes) and ultimately left the wipers sweeping annoyingly for the next thirty miles.

Whenever I changed lanes on I-70, a series of bells sounded and a weird voice behind the dash warned me to pull over and rest. I was aware that even a full semester at MIT would never prepare me to learn how to turn off that voice. I wondered if—whoever he was—he might have been preparing to shut down the Explorer's engine from a drone and produce a SWAT team to force me to rest, right there in the middle lane of the most dangerous stretch of interstate highway in all of America.

If you have ever been in a special Edition Ford Explorer, you will have noted that the number of digital displays on the dashboard is comparable to the Star Ship Enterprise. Even if you were to spend five hours studying the 350-page manual (loosely written in English, but with Japanese syntax), you could never master all the quirky icons on the dash waiting to be clicked while you hurtled in the dark at eighty miles per hour.

After surviving one night in a "condo" that had no windows, my technophilic young friend, Erik, remotely assisted me in undoing my inadvertent renting of two Airbnb units at the same time. I had accomplished those transactions when trying to upload my photo while two windows were open, completing an irreversible loop in an algorithm that was about to deposit my money in two different bank accounts.

The next day, I set off confidently to my Airbnb. The online directions took me to a complex called Snow Lion (there is actually no such thing as a snow lion, although there is such a thing as a snow tiger), where there were assigned parking slots for all the condos except one: Unit 208 (mine). After a few tries, I got an Airbnb manager on the phone. She told me that she would send me a link to lead me to the correct parking area. I told her I was in a giant Explorer and lacked Wi-Fi contact, unless I could figure out the dozens of programmable LED windows in the Explorer. Instead, we agreed that she would access the condo complex on Google Earth in her office (she was in Denver and had never been to the condo, or even to Vail, for that matter) and talk me in. She told me to turn into a lot two hundred yards after the red fire hydrant. That was sound advice, except there were a half dozen red fire hydrants ahead of me. After a few missteps, I found the correct lot and parked the Explorer in the one remaining space, which was marked "compact only."

I lugged my suitcase up three flights of stairs and only then realized that I hadn't memorized the four-digit code to the electronic door lock of Unit 208. But if I could go back to the lot, figure out the Explorer's Wi-Fi hotspot, log in to my email, and find the correct link, all would be well. But wait! Maybe I shouldn't be looking for an email—the code might have been sent in one of the twenty-seven Airbnb texts I had received. By the way, such texts are not to be confused with regular text messages, which are considered to be in an entirely different family. In the Explorer, I plugged my iPad Lightning Cable into the USB slot. Unsurprisingly, a pop-up said, "That USB connection is not supported. Disconnect immediately!"

Listen to me! I honestly cannot remember how I found the code. I was in what psychiatrists call a "fugue state." It is possible that I tried all ten thousand possible four-digit combinations on the lock. Or I simply guessed it on the first try. Maybe I went somewhere that had Wi-Fi hotspot availability? I wouldn't know.

Upon entering Unit 208, I felt the exact sense of triumph that Alex Hannold experienced after his solo free climb of El Capitan.

The temperature in the Vail Valley is very pleasant during the day in October, but it dips into the forties at night. Upon entering, it was chilly in the condo, so I went looking for the thermostat. I felt a sense of apprehension when I noticed that there were four buttons on the left of the device, vertically arranged, and five buttons on the bottom of it, horizontally arranged. But no matter how many buttons I pushed in random patterns, the little display screen remained dark. Aiming my iPhone flashlight (which has been stuck on strobe mode for about a year) at the device and squinting through my reading glasses, I discerned a tiny message in the upper right corner of the screen that was barely visible. It may have said, "Low battery."

I did not have any AA batteries in my possession at that moment, but, incredibly, a bearded man with a trucker hat was walking down the hall, and he happened to have some. Together, we pried off the front of the device with a screwdriver since it wouldn't come off otherwise. With the input of fresh voltage, the screen came alive, and I contemplated the nine flashing LED columns with names like "hold" and "run."

Realizing that I will never be smart enough to sort out a thing like that on my own, I opened my iPad and hunted for the condo's Wi-Fi name and password. Incredibly, I found them among the twenty-seven not-exactly texts from Airbnb and proceeded to open up YouTube. A very pleasant, diminutive gentleman from India with a squeaky voice provided a nice twelve-minute video on how to operate a Honeywell thermostat. If I could just summon the necessary mental focus, I would need to program four different "modes" on the device, each of which required setting three "functions." Any errors would require starting over. After some practice, I entered data for each of the four thermostat settings, correctly inputting time, date, and temperature for the four modes. I then pressed "run" to "lock it all in," as the gentleman from Mumbai had taught me. For simplicity, I chose seventy degrees for each of the modes.

When I woke up sweating at three o'clock in the morning, the condo's "smart thermostat" read seventy-seven.

For some reason, I went through a lot of dishes in the first couple of days I was there. I rinsed them and loaded up the dishwasher. I found some dishwasher soap and got ready to set the device in motion, noting that there were three choices for "wash," three choices for "dry," and three choices for something else that was not legible on the panel. The illegible word might have said "sani-something" or "delay start." Not so bad. Only nine permutations from which to choose, although results from the three settings dependent on the illegible button would remain a mystery and could cause me trouble down the line. After pressing all the buttons multiple times and checking the closure mechanism several times, nothing happened. Who knew? Maybe a previous tenant had programmed the thing for "one-month delayed start?"

I went back to YouTube and a diminutive Korean gentleman—equally pleasant—explained in less than nine minutes the various possibilities for operating a Frigidaire dishwasher. Most of the stuff looked familiar, except for a comment at the very end.

That was when he explained that you have to push the "start" button.

I got my strobe flashlight out and my reading glasses, crouched on the floor on my knees, and looked carefully at the dishwasher's front panel. Nowhere did it say "start." It was an old machine, and I could see that some of the writing had worn off. Hoping not to have a seizure induced by the strobe light, I thought I might be able to identify—way, way over to the right—a tiny, faint *S*, then a blank space followed by what could have been a *T*. I pressed that general area, and the machine leapt to life. Satisfaction!

Well, I figured I had mastered enough new technology to last me for a while, so I left the Roku TV for a later date. When I turned it on a few days later, I realized that every streaming service, sporting event, and essentially all of the one thousand-plus stations were unwatchable. None of them worked without the owner of the unit investing in upgrades to dozens of arcane packages and bundles.

I decided to read a book.

ORANGE PEPPER

I am guessing that most of you have had a black sheep in your family or still have one. When my dear cousin, Glen, was struggling with the cancer that eventually took his life, I wanted to write a silly story about him to make him laugh. It did. I also wanted to convey to him how much he was loved. It did that, also. In his honor, I now share the story with you.

As kids, we often walked through Coburn Cemetery, which abutted Grandma and Grandad's property on a gentle knoll overlooking Lake Mauweehoo in the rolling hills of western Connecticut. Most of the headstones in the ancient burial ground were very old, some dating from colonial times and the Civil War. The names on some of the monuments were no longer legible due to the erosive effects of acid rain on slate and granite over time.

One summer day, as I wandered through the graveyard with my younger cousin, Glen, then thirteen or fourteen years old, we noticed a cluster of stones memorializing a family named the Peppers. That got our attention because we knew some living members of the Pepper family.

They owned a small horse ranch at the other end of the lake called Memory Lane Farm, and I had recently painted their house and barns as a summer job, dodging swarms of hornets alongside a retired New York television personality known as Sheriff Bob Dixon. As Glen and I studied the inscriptions on the timeworn stones, one name gave us pause: *Orange Pepper*. His dates of birth and death were impossible to read. In the half-baked minds of two teenagers, the name seemed quite hilarious, and we giggled inappropriately by Mr. Pepper's grave. Why would anybody name their child after a citrus fruit and a spice?

Grandma Gardner favored me for reasons not entirely clear. Maybe it had to do with the fact that I tended to color within the lines, unlike Glen. Or the fact that he didn't like her lima bean casserole. In any case, Grandma doted on me. She even allowed me to drive her car, although I had only recently passed the driving test in Boston, where turn signals are a sign of weakness. At sixteen, taking the wheel of the white Mercedes-Benz with its royal blue plates was an intoxicating experience. Oddly, the car had no radio, but I still enjoyed cruising the freshly blacktopped country roads of Sherman. Occasionally, Grandma would allow me to drive myself into nearby New Milford to perform errands and pick up Breyer's ice cream and Hires root beer in heavy glass bottles at the A&P. On one of those outings, she directed me to get gasoline and gave me her Texaco credit card.

In those days, filling stations had *gas jockeys* who pumped the gas for you, raised the hood to check the oil, and washed the windshield with big squeegees. My jockey was a pimply kid, with grease-stained overalls and a shiny metal coin dispenser on his belt. He looked at me suspiciously when I said, "Fill'er up." Apparently, I didn't fit his image of someone who belonged behind the wheel of a German luxury car. But after I told him about being Grandma's favorite, he took the credit card and proceeded to top off the tank. A few minutes later, he presented me with a little receipt to sign, a waxy rectangular sheet of paper with two carbon copies aligned underneath it. He had imprinted the stack of slips with Grandma's credit card using a gadget known to gas jockeys everywhere as a "knuckle buster." He presented it to me through the driver's window on a little tray that was supposed to make it easier to record your signature with an oily Bic pen.

I signed in the space provided: *Orange Pepper.*

The signature was a bit of foolishness that didn't involve any thought process. I was pretty sure, anyway, that in the history of the Nutmeg State, very few souls had ever bothered to scrutinize those smeared little receipts, if and when they were ever mailed out to the cardholder at the end of the month.

About five weeks later, a neighborhood boy who did odd jobs parked his bike in the Gardners' driveway and brought up the mail and newspapers to Grandma, who was smoking a 100-millimeter menthol cigarette on her front porch. It wasn't a grand place, but from that porch, the view of Lake Mauweehoo and the surrounding hills was stunning. Built in 1908, using native fieldstones flecked with mica, the home we affectionately called "Greyrocks" was a cherished haven for three generations of our family.

Grandma handed the lad a quarter for his trouble, pretty good money for a youngster in those days, and he whistled as he pedaled down Leach Hollow Road on his single-speed Schwinn, a bike coveted by a generation of kids who had seen it in scores of Captain Kangaroo commercials. Its big wicker basket bulged with additional copies of the *New York Times*, *The New York Daily News*, and *Danbury News-Times.*

As Grandma leafed through the mail, she pulled out a bill with a Texaco star on the envelope.

ORANGE PEPPER

Thinking back on it, there may have been an exact moment in time when Grandma's respective impressions of Glen and me began to diverge some eight years earlier. She and Granddaddy Gardner had orchestrated an extravagant Christmas celebration for their grandchildren that year at Greyrocks. Our pediatric quartet included Glen, his sisters Donna and Sandy, and me. We ranged in age from about four to eight, with me in the role of the senior statesman. Glen was a chipper little fellow with an innocent demeanor vaguely suggestive of Theodore Cleaver. And, like "the Beave," he had a prominent impish streak. His huge upper incisors were erupting asymmetrically, separated by a gap of a quarter of an inch. His green and white holiday sweater featured hundreds of snowflakes below two bull moose regarding each other suspiciously.

Grandma was a frugal but loving woman. For some reason, she pulled out all the stops that year in an effort to obtain every item on the four wish lists we had mailed to the North Pole a few weeks earlier. With snow gently falling on the frozen expanse of Lake Mauweehoo and a fire crackling in the big living room fireplace through which Santa had recently descended, Sandy, Donna, and

I took turns opening our gifts, which had been lovingly wrapped in shiny green paper accessorized with rustic sprigs of pine. Satisfied for the most part with our largesse, we gathered around Grandma's balsam fir Christmas tree and turned the stage over to Glen, who was nearly bursting out of his pajamas with anticipation. He knelt behind an enormous heap of presents and shouted, "Everybody, get away! I'm opening!"

My memory for the next few minutes is the tiniest bit foggy now, but as Grandma and Granddad observed him keenly, let's just say that Glen had some *serious* opening to do, and he did it in a kind of manic frenzy. His haul included a model train set, a hockey stick, a catcher's mitt, a miniature football, four Matchbox cars, twenty-five tin soldiers, a Hula-Hoop, a toboggan, Mr. and Mrs. Potato Head, a Frisbee, a container of Silly Putty, a Slinky, a red cowboy hat with a satin band, and a toy drum. I might be missing one or two things.

When Glen had torn open the last of the presents, he was pensive for a moment before looking forlornly up at our grandmother. With an expression somewhere between incredulity and apoplexy, he asked, "Is this all I get?"

For her fifth birthday, Sandy received a card containing five dollars from our Great Aunt Florence, along with donations and endowments from a few other sources. Gathering the loot, she headed for Lester's grocery store, anxious to enact the master plan she had been refining for several months. Her objective—her holy grail, if you will—was to obtain two cases of a flavored drink mix called Funny Face, Kool-Aid's primary competitor. Each case contained twenty-four packets of the powdery treats, whose flavor became more complex, crisp, and fruity with the addition of water and a humongous amount of sugar. A short while later, loaded up with Rootin' Tootin' Raspberry, Freckle Face Strawberry, Choo Choo Cherry, and Goofy Grape, the youngster set out for home, ready to get down to work, with Glen acting as her wingman.

Sandy's understanding of plumbing was sound for a girl her age. She intuitively grasped the basics of fluid dynamics, including the nuances of laminar and turbulent flow. *Wouldn't it be delightful*, she imagined, *if a girl could enjoy a glass of Rootin' Tootin' any old time she wanted, just by going to the sink and turning on the faucet?* Toward that end, shouldn't it be possible to go to the water's source and create a permanent supply of the delicacy by simply emptying a massive quantity of the colorful powders into the little well next to the house that supplied the family's H2O?

The next morning, Sandy's dad, Joe, was taking a leak in the small bathroom on the second floor of their antique colonial home on Spring Lake Road. Sun splashed through the window, and mockingbirds and cardinals were singing on apple trees out back. It seemed like a promising morning until Joe flushed the toilet, looked down, and wondered why he was peeing purple. Thinking that there might be something wrong with his eyes, he went to the sink to rinse his face. Purple again—with some raspberry highlights. This was long before Jimi Hendrix created "Purple Haze" and Prince created "Purple Rain," but it probably felt like something psychedelic was going on. Joe rushed outside wearing pajama bottoms and a backward and inside-out T-shirt to see if the pipe from the well had been compromised by ionizing radiation from an underground deposit of uranium or radon. Or could it be something more occult?

About that time, Sandy decided to fess up and approached her dad at the well. Joe couldn't quite believe the story until Sandy pointed to a trash can bursting with empty packets of Rootin' Tootin' Raspberry, Freckle Face Strawberry, Choo Choo Cherry, and Goofy Grape.

Joe's mood began to shift from annoyance to amusement. Even so, Sandy decided that the better part of valor was, in her words, "To make myself scarce for a bit."

Glen had a generally positive experience at the tiny Sherman school. He and his sisters typically rode the school bus driven by Mr. Biggerstaff, a man who wore his fraying faux alligator belt above a bulging paunch, qualifying him as a "high waister" in Glen's parlance. For some reason, the old man had it in for Glen (or so Glen thought) and scrutinized him menacingly in the bus's rearview mirror whenever Glen was engaged in juvenile antics in the back row, which was all the time, more or less. Sandy sat behind the driver because "that's where the heat was." Donna sat up front, too, until Mr. B ran over an orange tiger cat, got out of the bus, and callously kicked the carcass off the road. After that, she sat further back. Glen considered Biggerstaff a "generally miserable guy" and an "ugly old turd" and avoided him by riding his bike to school in the warmer months.

For most of the year, however, Sherman's Rhodes Scholars (I'm teasing! Rhodes was their family surname), by the sheer accident of geography, were the first ones on the bus in the morning and the last ones off in the afternoon. Accordingly, they set, and still hold, the Connecticut state record for the most lifetime hours spent singing "Ninety-Nine Bottles of.Beer on the Wall" in a yellow seventeen-ton Blue Bird school bus.

There were thirteen kids in Glen's entire class. For a couple of years, he had a teacher named Gilda Clampitt, who greeted her students each day with gushy hugs and what she called "Eskimo kisses," meaning rubbing noses. Of course, Glen's favorite period was recess, where he excelled at kickball.

ADHD had not formally made its way into the understanding of early childhood development, so Glen was simply regarded as "hyper." In the later grades, he was involved in a number of classroom kerfuffles, a few relating to his persistent snapping of the straps of girls' training bras. There were some early romantic adventures, too, one involving a girl named Lynn Montina who enjoyed kissing. Besides the kissing, Glen only recalls that "her hip bones protruded."

One day, Sandy decided to create a set of contact lenses for herself in Mr. Hartshorne's classroom, who was also the school principal. Using a paper punch and Scotch tape, she applied the circular pieces of gluey tape directly to her eyeballs. After Hartshorne called her mother, Priscilla, Sandy was brought to an ophthalmology office to sort things out and was advised to leave contact lens design to the experts. (Around the same time, Sandy managed to glue her tongue to an iron railing outside the Rhodes' house, which had a frosty coating of snow that looked inviting. Priscilla was able to unstick the tongue with some warm water after an unnerving minute or two.)

Later on, Glen had a homeroom teacher named Missy Herrick. She wondered at times about Glen's grooming, even asking in a note to Joe and Priscilla, "How could a young boy get so dirty on the way to school?"

In a meeting with Principal Hartshorne, Missy described Glen as "The only student who could get dirty walking through a snowstorm."

Hartshorne agreed, adding, "The boy is a real-life version of Pigpen. He is a human soil bank who raises a cloud of dust on a perfectly clean street and passes out gumdrops that are invariably black."

"Last week, he came to school clean as a whistle and nobody recognized him," said Missy, as she returned to her classroom.

In a subsequent conference with his teacher, Glen objected to the Pigpen comparison, stating vehemently, "Mrs. Herrick, don't think of it as dirt. Just think of it as dust from far-off lands blowing over here and settling on me. I might be carrying soil that was trod upon by Solomon or Nebuchadnezzar or Genghis Khan. I wear the soot of countless ages, Mrs. H. Just think about it. It really staggers the imagination!"

Most of Sherman's youngsters stopped at Lester's Market, the only store in town, for popsicles, candy, and sodas after school. Not Glen. By seventh grade, the boy had developed a fondness for shrimp cocktail! Parking his banana bike on the side of the old market, he would head for the appetizer cooler and ignore the crab dumplings and pigs in a blanket in favor of the glass three-packs of his favorite hors d'oeuvre. Each of the glasses contained eight to ten nanoscopic crustaceans smothered in cocktail sauce, heavy on the horseradish. Taking full advantage of the Rhodes' good credit with Lester, Glen would emerge with the treats and somehow consume them before furiously pedaling past the town library and Gidding's Garage, as villagers pondered the red streaks dripping from the corners of his mouth. By the time Priscilla caught on, the family's monthly bill at the old store had about doubled.

For about two years, in early adolescence, Glen lived in a chicken coop. Presumably, this relocation from the family home stemmed from hormonal changes and anatomical developments in Sandy and Donna that required some distancing from their brother. As far as Glen was concerned, however, the new situation was "absolutely groovy." The coop, right across Spring Lake Road from the Rhodes' house, measured eight by fifteen feet and had a peaked roof. Not a palatial dwelling by any means, but the boy was now the master of his domain. The rows of laying boxes that, in their earlier life, had encouraged hens to lay their eggs in a clean cubicle in relative peace and privacy now harbored underpants, socks, and shirts. An old feed bin held a pole and rod for garments that needed to hang. (What! Did Glen have a collection of three-piece suits?) Surfaces had been whitewashed, and the place was mostly free of mice. Opposite the single bed were a small desk and a large gas heater, so it was warm enough in winter. When micturition was necessary, it happened naturally enough en plein air, accounting for the yellow spatter patterns on some of the snow banks out back.

Following dinner with the family and an episode of *Rawhide* or *Perry Mason*, Glen would adjourn to his quarters. After considering doing some homework—and quickly discarding the idea—he would tune his radio to the raspy voice of Wolfman Jack on WNBC and await a maiden named Amanda as darkness settled upon Sherman. The nocturnal visitor from a mansion on the hill that had once been owned by the Rhodes family had chestnut hair and green eyes.

A few hours hence, as the adolescent bachelorette headed back up the hill, Glen would drift off under his warm covers, channeling Paul Simon . . .

I got no deeds to do, no promises to keep
I'm dappled and drowsy and ready to sleep
Let the morning time drop all its petals on me
Life, I love you, all is groovy.

During those formative years, Glen hung around his dad's big woodworking shop from time to time. In a beautiful red barn at the northern edge of Spring Lake, Joe Rhodes and his crew created American and French provincial furniture as well as handcrafted pews and altars for churches. An assistant in the shop was a diminutive carpenter by the name of Pike Duncan. Pike was known for his exuberant cursing and for the use of his fists in bare-knuckle fighting at the Danbury Fair. His hair-trigger temper was legendary in a number of local watering holes, where, at the slightest hint of a challenge, he was ready to scuffle. "There was no backing off in Pike," said one childhood friend. While he—somewhat improbably—enjoyed croquet and clam bakes, Pike's distinguishing feature was the instinct to fight. Some of that had to do with his intolerance of bullies picking on someone weaker.

Pike was fond of little Glen. When Glen and Sandy broke into Pike's house and ate a chocolate cake that his wife, Sally, had just baked, Pike elected not to beat Glen to death.

Over the years, Pike "taught" Glen to swear. On a visit to Greyrocks at the age of nine, Glen displayed some of that colorful language. Granddaddy Gardner, a pretty conservative guy and man of few words, was tinkering in the garage that day. Wandering into Granddaddy's modest workshop, Glen heard his silver-haired grandfather whistling up in a loft. Glen gazed up curiously and bellowed, "What the hell's going on up there?"

As a youngster, Glen loved to ride his bike down Spring Lake Road to Andrew Morren's farm. "Andy" embodied the core values of a man who produces something of value from the land: accountability, integrity, and fairness. He was a wiry man whose weathered face featured impossibly bushy eyebrows, a beak-like nose, and giant ears that protruded at a ninety-degree angle from his head. Appropriately enough, his middle name was *Gump*. Glen learned about Andy's belief system while spreading manure, cleaning the barn, "picking rocks," and riding a tractor. He seemed to enjoy the chores and the simple meals that followed, listening attentively to Andy, his wife Shirley, and Grammy Morren as they discussed the news of the day. (Grammy, incidentally, obtained some of that news by covertly listening to her neighbors on the open party line, which—as weird as it seems today—was a landline shared among the residents of Spring Lake Road on which it was possible to quietly eavesdrop.) While Andy's approach to dairy farming was unusual in some ways—milking the cows at 11 a.m.—he was an attentive neighbor and friend. In the evening, he and Glen listened to a radio program called "Mystery Moment" in the barn while finishing chores. Glen's father, Joe, was elusive and emotionally distant. In his hours at the farm, Glen found a kind of surrogate father.

As positive as Glen's experience was at Andy's, he did endure one humbling experience that began in the milk house. The Berry brothers, a couple of adolescent wise guys, were working part-time at the farm. Taking advantage of Glen's wholesome nature and the certainty that he was not a candidate for the National Spelling Bee, one of the boys offered to "decorate" Glen's plain white T-shirt with a marker pen. Assuring Glen that the ornamentation would impress his friends and, especially, girls, the juvenile miscreant spread the shirt out on the cool milk tank and inscribed the word "ANUS" in bold capital letters across the front. Glen proudly donned the shirt and rode off into town, wondering why he was receiving strange looks. While stopping at Sherman's general store for shrimp cocktail, proprietor Lester Bennet took Glen aside and explained what the staring, sniggering, and tee-heeing was all about.

Postscript: The Berry brothers practiced additional mischief well into young adulthood and beyond. One spring, when Grandma and Granddad Gardner came home to Greyrocks after a winter in Delray Beach, Florida, the silver was gone. Guess who?

Many folks in Sherman consider a ninety-two-acre farm on Taber Road to be the jewel of their community. The property known as Happy Acres is a living symbol of the town's agricultural past. The fields where Black Angus and Hereford cattle graze today were maintained for most of the twentieth century by the Hapanowich family. For decades, the Christmas season in Sherman officially began when the family lit a huge star atop the farm's main silo. Overseeing the dairy and beef operations until his death at age eighty-five was a blond, muscular scion of the family named Anthony. For the villagers of Sherman, it was a lot easier to call him *Tony Happy*, and that sobriquet fit the man perfectly.

Throughout his school years, Glen made some pocket money by working at the big dairy farm, which straddled the road to Gaylordsville. He performed many of the same tasks he did at Andy Morren's place and tended to huge silage piles in a big field they called Bull Meadows. In Tony Happy, a man he affectionately referred to as "the Polack," Glen noticed many of the same qualities he admired in Andy Morren.

One winter, during the bird hunting season, Glen seized the chance to impose some frontier justice on Tony's behalf. Constitutionally intolerant of thoughtless behavior, Glen's sense of right and wrong was provoked when a hunter parked his pick-up and set off on Tony's property without asking for the farmer's permission. *Trespassing*, by definition. After happening upon the offending vehicle,

Glen hooked up a giant manure spreader with a gearbox full of corn head grease and engaged the tractor's power take-off. Sprockets sprang to life, flail beaters began shredding, and the drag chain conveyors started sweeping. When the curved tines of the iron forks commenced scooping, Glen skillfully maneuvered the controls and deposited 145 bushels of pungent manure on the hood and roof of the hunter's truck.

Later that day, two stony-faced state troopers appeared at Tony's door with an arrest warrant for Glen and a list of criminal complaints. The case was referred to the Danbury District Court and assigned to a Superior Court Judge who was small in stature and preferred not to use his first name, which was Treat. Within the Connecticut justice system, Judge T. Clark Hull was known for a mischievous sense of humor—rather unusual in the lofty realms of jurisprudence—as well as a style of decision-making based on what he felt was "best for Joe Lunchbox." As it turned out, those idiosyncrasies made him an ideal candidate to hear Glen's case.

Judge Hull first considered the motive behind Glen's use of the Hapanowich "meadow muffins" to reprimand the grouse hunter. He concluded that, beyond any question, the intent was a righteous one. Considering next the weapon used in the alleged crime, the jurist apparently couldn't suppress a chuckle, recognizing the impeccable symbolism of the noxious droppings as Glen's artillery of choice.

After carefully weighing the evidence, Judge T. Clark Hull elected to acquit Glen on all charges, including felony disposal of excrement, misdemeanor assault with crapola, malicious mischief with night soil, creating a nuisance with doo-doo, buffalo chip bullying, dissing with dung, turd terror, harassment with guano, battery with number two, and disorderly ca-ca-conduct.

Glen went back to work.

Interestingly, most rural communities in the 1950s had a "town drunk." In the early television series *The Andy Griffith Show*, the town of Mayberry had Otis Campbell. Sherman had a diminutive, unkempt fellow by the name of Melvin Penrose, who wore coveralls, swore copiously in Polish, and lived with his mother. Presumably, the coveralls protected him from any biological, chemical, or thermal hazards he was worried about in rural Connecticut. The boiler suit also had a special pocket reserved for a tin of Copenhagen dipping tobacco. Melvin's face typically had a flushed hue under three or four days of stubble.

Melvin's favorite libation, Ballantine ale, was brewed from the waters of the Passaic River in Newark, New Jersey, known for its "sewage overflow events" and persistently elevated levels of dioxin, mercury, lead, arsenic, pesticides, and radioactive strontium.

When healthy (How often could that have been?), he worked for the town, cutting the high grass along the main thoroughfares with a wooden scythe, not unlike the one wielded by the Grim Reaper. A physical job like that had to be challenging for a man who habitually woke up with agitation, global confusion, visual and auditory hallucinations, flatulence, persistent sexual arousal, tactile sensations of crawling insects, fever, high blood pressure, nausea, a peculiar impression that his teeth were itching, intractable hiccups, intense sweating, and a troubling sense that his liver was "wobbling." On "bad days," Melvin also struggled with an irresistible impulse to throw compacted pellets of his feces at total strangers.

When Glen was a toddler, Melvin ran him over in a maroon '52 Chevy sedan. According to Sandy, Glen was chasing a rabbit and ran onto Spring Lake Road. Sandy noticed a car veering erratically in their direction, realized that Melvin was at the wheel, and yelled—but it was too late. Melvin hit Glen and dragged him under his car for a considerable distance. To this day, for his trouble,

Glen has an indentation in the back of his skull that is free of hair.

The degree to which Melvin was impaired was unclear, but when he exited the sedan to see what he had hit, his breath smelled more like cat litter than strawberries, suggesting serum ketone levels too high to be measured and generally inconsistent with life.

The Rhodes kids were understandably unhappy with Melvin after the accident and heckled him whenever the chance arose. They were aware that, each and every afternoon, Sherman's hophead would hole up in a big tobacco barn on his property, where—surrounded by mountainous piles of empty green cans with the iconic XXX Ballantine logo—he would drink himself into oblivion. Perhaps regarding himself as Sherman's Tobacco King or Emperor of Ale, Melvin would ensconce himself in a big wicker chair in the middle of the "hanging room." Bracketed by floor-to-ceiling sheets of curing tobacco leaves that hung like serrated green curtains around his throne, Melvin would proceed to blow his mind with the fermenting byproducts of hops, barley, and yeast.

When the mountain of cans in the shed made it impossible to even walk safely, Melvin would throw vast quantities of the empties into the woods. On top of everything else, an environmentalist Melvin was not.

When they had nothing better to do, Sandy, Glen, and Donna would head over to Melvin's farm after school and choreograph a little mischief. The kids were familiar with Melvin's routine and knew that he typically chugged exactly one hundred forty-four ounces (a dozen jumbo cans) of the Passaic lager before emerging from the barn to lock up and stagger to the house. Accordingly, when Melvin was about halfway to the domicile, the Rhodes siblings would toss rocks at the enormous shed from their hiding place in a nearby culvert. Spinning around with a baffled look, red-faced and drunk as a skunk, Melvin would lurch back to the barn and unlock it, searching for vandals and cursing. Finding nobody there, he would fumble with the lock again before weaving back toward the house, repeatedly muttering an expletive in Polish that sounded like *Pascallioshki, Pascallioshki, Pascallioshki!*

For Sandy, Glen, and Donna, the challenge was to see how many times they could get Melvin to flounder back to the barn, having literally forgotten that he had just been there. It was incredible that a man could be that drunk, but Melvin had had a lot of practice and was probably suffering from the neurological condition known to medical interns everywhere as "squash rot."

After eight years at the Sherman school, Glen spent a year boarding at a small private school in the town of Washington, Connecticut, called Rumsey Hall. Wearing a blue blazer and necktie, however, never felt quite right, and he had a hard time relating to boys who were dropped off in limousines at the start of the semester. Like others of us in the family, Glen had friends in *low* places and enjoyed them thoroughly. One math teacher and athletic coach at Rumsey, Lou Magnolia, believed strongly in Glen and encouraged him to stay. But, in the end, he was more comfortable moving on to New Milford High School as a sophomore.

By his own admission, Glen was not much of a student there, but he was a good athlete. As a star fullback at New Milford, he was willing to carry the ball when the other running backs had tired of being gang-tackled by superior teams. When the football season ended, however, Glen determined that there was more fun in smoking pot and racing cars than there was in getting gang-tackled by the New Fairfield Rebels' bloodthirsty linebackers. He also showed very little interest in figuring out the square root of pi in math class.

Glen's primary interests made a lot of noise, went fast, or both. His '65 Chevy two-tone Impala was maroon and beige. Under its hood were four hundred and twenty-seven cubic inches of internal combustion, volumetric displacement, expanding gases, and unapologetic manliness. And, happily, a number of his female classmates were intrigued by the car's massive cylinder block and Glen's own rigid drive shaft that produced lavish amounts of torque, stroke, and bore.

In those months, it was not unusual for the good folks of Sherman and their resident state trooper to experience increasing levels of exasperation at the sight of fresh burn-out marks on the long straightaway on Route 39, a perfect venue for drag racing.

At the time, Glen had an interest in one of the bevy of girls in the Robertson family. After his weekend shifts at Tony Happy's, he would typically head over to see Susie at the family's home on Candlewood Lake, where Mrs. Robertson (Betty) playfully accused him of bringing flies into the house from the farm. The Robertsons loved Glen despite the fact that he smelled like manure much of the time.

During that summer, a once-in-a-generation infestation of a pest called *Malacosoma americium*—"tent caterpillars"—occurred in western Connecticut. Each day for two weeks, thousands of squishy moth larvae dropped from the limbs of the leafy trees in the Robertsons' yard and fell onto their steep driveway, creating a gooey surface layer of slime. When Glen showed up one evening to pick up Susie, the Impala fishtailed on the fungal goop, lurching precariously toward the lake as Glen struggled to regain traction. After watching him emerge from the Chevy at the bottom of the yucky incline, Betty gently encouraged him to avoid tracking the goo into her domicile.

Around the time of graduation, Glen was offered a job as a kind of private detective. This seemed like a natural career fit for someone who had watched hundreds of hours of *Matlock, Kojak, Columbo, Mannix, The Rockford Files, Starsky and Hutch, Cannon, Banacek, Get Smart, The Girl From U.N.C.L.E., Hawaii Five-O, Mission Impossible,* and, most importantly, *The Mod Squad.* His assignment was to catch dishonest employees who were stealing from retail car parts stores in the region. It involved a kind of good cop, bad cop routine that he perfected with a friend named Dayne Dukes. During that period of time, Glen acquired a Triumph 650 motorcycle and occasionally raced it after work on the runways of the Danbury Airport late at night when the facility had closed for the day.

There was a memorable occasion one summer that brought the Triumph and Granddaddy Gardner into some conflict. On a sultry August day, Granddad arranged to have the driveway at Greyrocks repaved. Our silver-haired patriarch took particular pride in the appearance of his dooryard and loved the look of a pristine blacktop surface after it had been rolled to smooth perfection. By chance, Glen chose that very day for a visit to his grandparents.

He appeared on his bike from the direction of Danbury and roared down Leach Hollow Road toward Greyrocks, shattering windows in the Mauweehoo Club and nearly bursting the eardrums of an unlucky letter carrier whose van was idling by the mailbox. As he accelerated up the driveway and downshifted, Grandma Gardner, who was smoking a 100-millimeter Benson and Hedges on the porch, covered her ears and muttered, "My God, that's awful!"

After imbibing two of Grandma's root beer floats, some cucumber slices in a bowl of vinegar, a heavily salted radish, and a few scallions, Glen departed on the Harley. As the bike emitted its iconic, ear-splitting *Vroom* and rasping, syncopated vibration, Grandma again covered her ears and mumbled, "My God, that's awful!"

A bit later, Granddad strolled down to admire the driveway with its immaculate new blacktop. He was stunned to find two massive parallel divots in the driveway, compliments of Glen's kickstand. The forlorn look on Granddaddy's face was a sad thing, and even after the vandalism was repaired, Granddad's psychological damage lingered for a bit.

There was a brief period of time during which all three Rhodes kids lived together in "The Little House." The charming cottage was the carriage house of the former Rhodes estate that featured a sprawling stone mansion high up on the hill. Thankfully for Sandy, Glen, and

Donna, The Little House and acres of adjacent fields remained in the family. In the spirit of "good, clean fun" one night, the teens acquired a tank of nitrous oxide from their friend Fat Bob (who was improbably able to purchase it at a welding supply store) and filled fifty five-gallon garbage bags with the colorless "laughing gas" using a segment of a garden hose.

When their father popped in unannounced, Joe found his children convulsed in paroxysms of giggling as they hugged the massive Hefty bags with shit-eating grins. Speaking unintelligibly in unnatural voices, they resembled a deranged glee club from outer space.

Joe took in the scene for a moment, mumbled, "*What the fuck?*" under his breath, and exited The Little House without another word.

After Glen's run as a private eye, the time came for some longer-term career planning. One thing he knew for sure was that he would rather suck eggs than spend the next four decades sitting in a cubicle in an office building. Like the Dixie Chicks, he was more inclined toward wide open spaces. Furthermore, he had figured out that he was temperamentally more suited to serving as his own boss than following the orders of a pimply administrator in a polyester suit and revolting necktie.

Unlike Robert Frost, Glen never described the woods as "lovely." Not his kind of adjective. But I believe it's fair to say that, in the depths of a New England hardwood forest alongside his pit bull, Ezra, he discovered a kind of spiritual sanctuary, one in which "even the deer felt safe." As a woodsman, Glen would remove massive trees with loud machinery that, in the short term, would fracture the tranquility of the woods. But, in the long term, he saw logging, done well, as a way of respectfully "managing" a forest and leaving it healthier than he found it, including attracting more wildlife.

Furthermore—and importantly—in this endeavor, Glen got to operate humongous machines. Working with heavy equipment, including feller bunchers, stump grinders, and loaders, gave him considerable pleasure. There were only two or three occasions over the years when those titanic machines tore down cable and power lines, leaving the Sherman population temporarily without power and internet. Not too bad.

Over time, he and Ezra mastered the woodsman's craft, and both managed to retire without being crushed to smithereens by falling red oaks and hard maple.

Early on, while working on a logging job in a neighborhood appropriately called Timber Trails, Glen spotted a woman named Casey who was sunbathing. Sometime later, they were married and had two strapping sons named Colton and Galen. Glen resolved not to repeat his father's pattern of distance and restraint. He and his boys were close, sharing a passion for anything involving internal combustion, among other things.

Glen loves his pit bull D-O-G (*Dee-Oh-Gee*), so much that, even when she chewed on Glen's false teeth, the transgression was quickly forgiven. Glen had left the choppers in an accessible place. How was D-O-G supposed to know? D-O-G is one of several dogs that live with Glen and his patient second wife, Lucy.

There is an elementary school not far from their home. At recess, the unmistakable sounds of joy on a playground waft through the neighborhood. The high-pitched howling, jubilant screams, and uninhibited caterwauling combine into an unmistakable signal to D-O-G that children are nearby and having fun. Since D-O-G, like a Trader Joe's chicken, is a free-range animal—no leash for her—of course, she hustles over to the playground from time to time to check things out.

Unfortunately, pit bulls can appear intimidating to some people, and the school's safety control officer is one of them. On six occasions, that official reported D-O-G to the dog warden for an offense called "roaming." There was some mention, too, of "growling," which Glen found impossible to believe. Each ticket was worth $180, and, needless to say, Glen elected to ignore them as a matter of principle. When an additional three violations were issued for ignoring the dog warden's concerns about having an "unregistered animal," Glen's sense of moral justice became even more resolute. Glen would have liked to insult the man with a nasty remark like "You couldn't even be elected dog catcher" until he remembered that the fellow had already been elected dog catcher.

One evening, around supper time, Glen and Lucy heard unusual sounds coming from the garage. When Lucy went to investigate, she encountered two state police officers with broad-brimmed Stetson hats, blue uniforms, glossy jackboots, and a warrant for Glen's arrest.

After declining Glen's invitation to come in for a bite to eat, the officers explained that the law required them to handcuff him en route to the barracks in a place called Canaan (which I had previously thought of as the home of a biblical civilization of Semitic-speaking people targeted for extermination in the Book of Joshua).

After Glen changed out of his pajamas and collected his medications and insulin, the trio set off in a Ford Taurus. Deciding that Glen was unlikely to flee, the officers agreed to handcuff Glen's hands in front rather than behind his back. Glen put in a call to his friend, Dusty, who was known for keeping a supply of cash handy in the event of unforeseen developments just like this. When his cell phone rang with Dusty's return call, one of the officers had to awkwardly retrieve it from Glen's back pocket. Dusty had some cash, but not the whole amount, and besides, he was having a hard time believing that this whole thing wasn't some kind of elaborate prank by Glen.

At the barracks, fingerprinting was followed by a long wait. Eventually, Lucy was able to amass the $720 needed for Glen's unpaid tickets, bail, penalties, and fines, but not before the payment process was held up briefly when it turned out that exact change was required. Accordingly, she set off on a tour of the few convenience stores open at that hour. At about midnight, having grudgingly lost his stand-off with the criminal justice system, Glen escaped imprisonment and made it home.

D-O-G greeted him warmly.

For a time, Glen thought of himself as the village idiot.

After previously living in a chicken coop for two years, spending a few hours in one should have been a simple matter for him. At the very least, you could expect him to get in and out of one uneventfully. But *no*. This was January in New England, there was no source of heat in the coop, Glen was no longer a spring chicken—if you'll forgive that turn of phrase—and, in this case, the only exit was hermetically sealed by a fiendish lock.

Glen was taking care of his neighbors' animals on that fateful Saturday morning. Judy and Doug Neugold, who were vacationing in South Carolina, had a kind of miniature zoo that consisted primarily of animals they had rescued. On the day of Glen's incarceration, the menagerie included Charlotte the pig, Kahuna, the largest of five horses, two goats, and a dozen chickens. Judy referred to the animals as *pensioners*, meaning they were essentially retirees who would never have to worry about being sent to a slaughterhouse.

Glen started his routine that morning with the goateed billies in their pen. When he bent over with his back turned, a goat head-butted him in the behind. Was he establishing dominance, Glen wondered, or was that an expression of erotic interest? He then walked into the barn and took care of the five horses, including Judy's huge dapple-grey Percheron. Charlotte, too, knew food was coming and, not without effort, arose from her bed. Glen then passed through the adjoining tack room, which was heated, and entered the numbing cold of the chicken coop. Always conscious of his manliness, Glen equipped himself with a yellow plastic scoop before entering the domain of Judy's barnyard fowl. Not wanting the chickens to escape, he absentmindedly settled the latch into a wobbly striker plate on the door separating the tack room from the coop. After hearing a resounding click, he turned the handle and realized he had just locked himself inside the coop and out of the warmer reaches of the barn. The temperature in the coop was in the mid-teens.

For some reason, Glen had left his cozy jacket in the tack room. It was visible through the little windows in the heavy door, tantalizingly close, but now oh so far away. He didn't have his cell phone either, having left it in the little Kubota tractor he used to travel between the Neugolds' place and his. Besides having no real shovel, there were two reasons he couldn't dig himself out by tunneling under the mesh fencing that surrounded the chicken coop. First, the ground around the coop was frozen solid. Second, the fence had been constructed with mesh buried a foot or two underground so as to discourage digging predators like foxes and coyotes. There was no wire cutter to slash through the otherwise impenetrable screen walls. Yelling didn't do any good since the Nuegolds were away. And even if he could hurl himself like a stuntman through one of the screened panels, the chickens would escape.

In other words, Glen had ensnared himself in a glacial henhouse. The temperature was dropping, and there was no way out. The birds, while technically incarcerated like Glen, were comfortably warm with their thickened winter feathers and the little heat lamp that was mounted on their laying perch.

So, what did Glen think about during his internment? Most of his thoughts were forms of self-castigation: "What a fucking dummy!" "What a nincompoop!" "What a moron!" But, as the minutes of imprisonment slowly turned into hours, it became hard to think at all. A polar vortex was streaming air from the Arctic that was cold enough to make a man's gonads shrivel. Had D-O-G been there, at least Glen could have experienced a one-dog night (or morning, in this case), but she wasn't. (D-O-G has a very strong primal instinct to eat anything that clucks.) And, as anyone who has been in a chicken coop can attest, spending time with hens involves some good, some bad, and plenty of *smelly*.

After several hours, Lucy wondered what had become of her hubby. She strolled down from the Rhodes' house to

Doug and Judy's barn and walked around to the chicken coop. Behind the steel mesh of the enclosure, she noticed a whimpering figure staring into the distance with a deranged expression.

Looking closer, she recognized the trembling apparition whose hair and eyebrows were coated in permafrost.

"What the hell are you doing?" she asked.

Glen had, in fact, forgotten what he was doing due to progressive hypothermia. To Lucy, he looked like a man who had been cryogenically stored in a giant vat of liquid nitrogen at negative 196 degrees centigrade.

In Glen's brain, the hypothalamus sensed that it was cold enough to freeze the balls off a brass monkey and initiated a shivering reflex in an effort to generate heat. Quivering like a leaf, with tiny icicles hanging from his nostrils and the whites of his eyes rolled back at a grotesque angle, Glen looked not unlike Jack Torrance, the madman who freezes to death in the maze outside the Overlook Hotel in the final scene of *The Shining*.

Exiting the fowl deep freeze, Glen's speech was unintelligible. Lucy took her husband's arm, and they stumbled to the little Kubota for the short ride home and a period of rewarming and reflection. For a moment or two, Lucy expected Glen to channel Jack Torrance and announce, "Here's Johnny!" but, in fact, he was simply too cold to speak.

Sometime later, the same fate befell Doug and Judy's son, Evan, the star center of the Newfoundland Growlers hockey club. He, too, managed to lock himself in the coop. Accordingly, Glen felt a little less like a nitwit. Now, there were two numbskulls. A *pair* of village idiots.

By now, you're probably wondering what happened when Grandma Gardner opened the Texaco bill. In truth, I wasn't around on that splendid summer day on the porch at Greyrocks when Grandma took a puff of her 100-millimeter Benson and Hedges slim and opened the mail. After studying the waxy receipts, she grabbed a magnifying glass and commenced handwriting analysis. That was inconclusive, but—clearly—someone had stolen her credit card! And who the hell was this *Orange Pepper*?

After puzzling over the crime for a bit, Grandma gazed out over the lake, hoping for sudden clarity. Granddad appeared with a shaker of martinis but was otherwise unable to help. After considering a variety of possibilities, Edna's suspicion began to focus on Glen, the one grandchild known for perpetrating shenanigans. (She never gave a thought to the golden boy from Boston.)

Surely, Glen had stolen the credit card and replaced it. If, like Sherlock Holmes, you ruled out all the other possibilities, you were left with that conclusion. And maybe he had even stolen the Benz when nobody was watching. Answers were needed—now!

The phone rang at the Rhodes' house on the other side of town. Thirteen-year-old Glen had no idea what was coming when his mom, Priscilla, handed him the phone with a puzzled look.

"Glen, I know you stole my Texaco card. Just admit it," said Edna.

"I didn't do it. And, by the way, what are you talking about? It's no fun to be wrongly accused. Have you thought about the possibility that the culprit might be your pet grandson? That apple polishing, goody-goody, boot-licking, abstemious sycophant from Massachusetts?"

"Well, no, now that you mention it, I hadn't."

No, she hadn't. But eventually, the truth came out, as it sometimes does. Grandma paid the scandalous bill and told Glen she was sorry. Grandmother and grandson both learned a valuable lesson about the injustices that can result from typecasting. As for the golden boy from Massachusetts, he learned not to impersonate dead people.

After all this time, I'm not sure who the real Orange Pepper is. It could be Glen, and it could be me. It could be both of us or neither of us. What I do know is how glad I am to have him as my homey, my boy. I'm proud of him for a bunch of reasons. For starters, he took the road less traveled and traveled it in a variety of ginormous, internally combusting machines that would scare the shit out of most people.

He's been true to himself throughout his life, walking to the beat of his own drum, if you will, although he'd be more than happy if he could drum like his hero, Max Weinberg.

Glen is a loving parent and loyal friend. He ain't afraid to stand up for his beliefs, and if you mess with those beliefs, you know what will happen to you . . . *manure*! Unlike yours truly, Glen can also fix a lot of things, especially if the thing happens to have one or more pistons and requires grease. (By contrast, when my car runs out of window washer fluid, I speed dial AAA.) For better or worse, he's never been afraid to let you know how he feels about something. And he loves animals.

When he's dealt a setback, Glen deals with it and keeps on being his endearing, irascible, and combustible self.

And, luckily for him, his gracious Lucy has been at his side throughout what Zorba the Greek aptly described as the "full catastrophe" of a human life.

Keep on truckin', cousin! A lot of people love you.

I sure do.

AFTERWORD

Dear Reader,

This morning, I felt a little sad and wasn't quite sure why. Maybe I was experiencing a version of the feeling you get when you're coming to the end of something—in this case, finishing up a book. Perhaps I was subliminally remembering something my mom read to me from *Winnie the Pooh*. In the passage, Pooh says goodbye to Christopher Robin and describes how lucky he is to be sad because he has something that makes saying goodbye so hard. I hope that's the case here.

Most of us would agree that the times we live in right now are troubled. While writing these stories, it made me feel a little better when I took a moment to stop and marvel at the astonishing resilience of Izzy Arbeiter, the innate kindness of Sam Wood, the otherworldly bond of love between Joline and Brecken, and the seriously silly laughter of Camp Jabberwocky. If it's not too presumptuous of me, I hope the stories made you feel a little bit better, too.

It makes me happy to think that next spring, on the third Monday in April, 30,000 people from many walks of life will lace up sneakers and begin the daunting journey from Hopkinton, Massachusetts, to Boston. Along the way, half a million souls will cheer them on, passionately wanting every one of those athletes to cross the finish line. On Marathon Monday, Boston will once again be a metaphor for a world in which people from varied backgrounds believe that we can live in peace and support one another through the joys and challenges of life. A world in which none of us will ever face adversity alone.

With gratitude,

Doctor Steve

ACKNOWLEDGMENTS

I want to express my heartfelt gratitude to Bryan Heathman, Alice Kirkwood, and Emily Waltenburg at Made for Success for their consistent encouragement and thoughtful guidance in nurturing this book into reality. And to their design staff for making me *smile* each time I look at the book's wonderful cover.

I want to thank the people in the stories and their families for generously sharing highly personal experiences in their lives with me and, through me, with readers they will never know.

I thank the individuals who took the time to read excerpts from the manuscript and share their thoughts, including Wade Johnson, Joline Swartz, Sandra Rhodes, and Donna Johanson.

I owe a big debt of gratitude to Rabbi Lawrence Kushner for the inspiration in his writings, especially *Invisible Lines of Connection.*

Every day, I am amazed and inspired by the resilience and joy so poignantly exhibited by the people in these stories, not least of all, the campers and volunteers of Camp Jabberwocky and its sister camps, including Zeno Mountain Farm, the Ashmere Project, and the Wabe of Whidbey.

Finally, I thank my late son, Graham, for his very great gift of opening my mind and heart to a different way of looking at this world and the people in it.

GRACES

Like every primary care physician, I have seen innumerable patients struggle with depression and situational stress. Over time, I tried to find better ways to coach them on strategies to help themselves. Eventually, I decided to put those thoughts into a handout with an acronym in the title that was easy to remember. Here is the result, with hopes that you might find it useful.

One of life's harsh realities is that, sooner or later, all of us face sadness and loss. And—with equal certainty—we will be confronted by periods of stress and anxiety. In the best of times, we can expect to be confronted by those stressors. But it is hard to remain unaffected emotionally when we are relentlessly bombarded with dire warnings about climate change and graphic images of mutating viruses, mass shootings, and war.

Sometimes, symptoms of grief and anxiety are brief and manageable. But occasionally, they persist, become intrusive, and are more elusive to manage. In those cases, it is a good idea to talk to a physician or other health care provider and ask for assistance. It sometimes turns out that medication is useful, short-term or long-term, when symptoms are very severe and affect quality of life.

But, whether or not the strategies of counseling or medication are appropriate for a given individual, there is one absolute prerequisite we need to tap into if we want to feel better: We need to do everything in our power to help ourselves.

We all have the tools to do this. Some of them may be a bit rusty, or we may be hesitant to take them out of the figurative "tool kit" we haven't opened for a while. But when we are feeling poorly for more than a little while, we need to put all of our tools to use. Let's imagine for a moment that our tool chest has six sections, each marked by a letter. The letters spell out the word *GRACES.*

G. GIVING

The old maxim "those who give the most themselves become full" happens to be quite true. And this happy paradox is available to every one of us. Like boomerangs, gestures of kindness have a way of coming back around.

Even a tiny act of goodwill can set in motion an invisible wave of goodness that ripples out into the world. In time, some of the ripples will be reflected back to the one who set them in motion. For the person who throws a pebble of kindness into a pond, the returning ripples typically take the form of a very pleasant sensation, a feeling that might even be called "grace." Acts of compassion, no matter how small, are heartwarming for both donor and recipient. Shakespeare lyrically articulated this notion in *The Merchant of Venice*:

> *"The quality of mercy is not strain'd;*
> *It droppeth as the gentle rain from heaven*
> *Upon the place beneath. It is twice blest;*
> *It blesseth him that gives and him that takes."*

The idea that kindness can contribute to healing was articulated in another way a century ago by an alumnus of Harvard Medical School, Dr. Karl Menninger: "Love cures people, both the ones who give it and the ones who receive it."

When I see random acts of kindness by strangers in public places, I feel a subtle change in my brain chemistry. Something as small as seeing someone hold a door for a stranger can do it. Maybe an endocrinologist can explain that change in my state of mind based on levels of dopamine or endorphins. I don't know or really care. I just know that witnessing small acts of kindness affects me, and I always feel more cheerful and hopeful after seeing them.

Accordingly, when feeling overwhelmed or "blue" ourselves, doing something charitable for someone else can be restorative. It can be as simple as taking ten seconds to put an anonymous Post-it note on a colleague's desk, saying, "I feel really lucky to work with you." Or it can be as grand as starting a new charity to honor someone you love and promoting that cause with time and money. At Camp Jabberwocky, the sleepover camp on Martha's Vineyard for adults and children with disabilities, I have witnessed acts of compassion (some by individuals as young as fifteen) so stunning that I have often been left in a state of awe. My spirit in those moments is utterly transformed by witnessing what Dr. Menninger rightly called "love."

One night, I was driving home from work in Boston to my home north of the city in a cold, driving rain (a downpour that, at that moment, felt not at all like Shakespeare's "gentle rain"). About halfway home, a traffic light turned red and I skidded to a stop in the murky dusk, the car's wipers oscillating furiously. I was exhausted and frustrated by something that had happened at work that day and felt persecuted by the traffic and the weather.

Through irregular streaks in the foggy windshield, I spotted a very old man in a dilapidated wheelchair, hatless and utterly drenched, making his way across the highway as the pedestrian crossing clock ticked down toward zero. As I watched, one of the wheels on his chair caught in a rut in the road, and he began to visibly struggle, stranded suddenly in the middle of the busy highway. The man was nearly invisible in the misty deluge as scores of exasperated commuters behind me revved their engines in a kind of fight or flight state, waiting for the millisecond when the light would turn green.

I put on my emergency flashers, exited my car cautiously, holding up my arms like a traffic cop, and walked to the middle of the intersection. It was an easy job to tip the man's chair back a fraction and redirect it out of the rut—and off he sped, without a word. I was soaked when I got back to my car, but my mood had changed. I had forgotten whatever it was that was frustrating me. I felt less depleted and miserable for the duration of my commute. I even found myself smiling.

When we don't feel so great spiritually, we will always benefit from doing something to assist others. We can volunteer for an organization whose cause resonates with us, help out in a soup kitchen, run or walk to raise money for a charity, answer phones for a non-profit, or do any of a thousand other things that benefit someone else. The charity that we release in those moments will bring a heightened sense of goodwill right back to us—guaranteed.

Every one of us has something to offer, perhaps more than we realize. According to an African proverb, "Even the poorest person has something to give and the richest person has something to receive."

The kindest people I have ever met and marveled at over the years are also among the happiest people I know.

R. RECONNECTING

Entropy is a term that scientists use to describe the tendency of things to decline, degrade, or slowly collapse into disorder over time. Let's say that, on a crisp Saturday in October, I rake maple leaves in my back yard into a tidy round pile before leaving town for a week. Certainly, my neat little heap of leaves will no longer be so tidy when I return. Wind, rain, my neighbor's Alaskan Malamute, and a gaggle of children scuffing through the pile will inevitably scatter my work. At some point, in fact, there will no longer be a pile of leaves.

For better or worse, life is like that pile of leaves. As youngsters, everyone we know and care about is near to us. We grow up and laugh with those people and develop bonds with them. In my analogy, Bruce, my third-grade buddy who is great at shooting marbles, is one of the red maple leaves in my tidy pile. Marsha, who hosts spin-the-bottle parties in the old barn behind her house after school, is one of the gold leaves. Lisa, whom I will always have a painful crush on, is one of the flaming orange leaves. But, in just a few years, Bruce will have moved to Arizona when his father gets a promotion, Marsha will enroll in a private school two thousand miles away, and Lisa will entirely stop communicating with her old friends for reasons that elude us.

This social form of entropy tends to dissipate the powerful bonds of friendship and mutual support that strengthen our psyches when we are younger. This phenomenon is made even worse by the natural tendency of anxiety and sadness to create a feeling of isolation. It can be difficult to find the energy to stay in touch with special friends or family when we are feeling poorly, perhaps even feeling that other people don't want to be around us. Furthermore, the natural tendency over time is for friends to insidiously slip away into the progressively demanding lives of adults, with a perfect storm of careers, marriages (and divorces), children, financial pressures, and geographic moves conspiring to lessen our contact with them.

I would suggest, however, that being with old friends and loved ones is therapeutic, perhaps even essential to feeling well. The "ties that bind us" to people with whom we have shared both the sweetness and sorrows of life are crucial threads in our emotional well-being. Reconnecting with people who care about us leads to positive emotional experiences like reminiscing and laughing, which lessen the oppressive weight of anxiety and sadness.

The challenge, then, is to rake the maple leaves back into as much of a pile as possible. But doing so requires some actual work. Reconnecting is a challenge that requires initiative and perseverance. For it to work, we need to get over our inertia and take an active role in reigning those friends back into our social orbit. We need to get out the old address book or smartphone and do some homework if we want to rekindle a friendship that has been slipping away. It's not really all that hard, but it takes a conscious effort. Here's how we can do it:

We send one text a day, saying something like, "Bruce, I miss you, buddy! What do you say about planning a reunion the next time you are here on business?" We fire off an email a day, saying something like, "Marsha, I hate the thought of losing touch with you. I have Red Sox tickets next weekend. Can you and your husband join us?" And we can even get a big batch of old-fashioned postcards and put "forever" stamps on them and send one snail mail a day to a lost classmate from yesteryear, suggesting sharing a beer after work or a dinner. Maybe Lisa, the object of my fascination, will respond, and I will summon the courage to confess my feelings to her.

So here is the homework assignment: Take two minutes a day every day for the next week and send off a text, an email, and a postcard (right...all three) to three friends who have drifted away like leaves in the wind. Then, make those gestures a habit. It will take less time than brushing your teeth or paying your bills, and it will surely help reclaim some of the friendship, mutual support, and laughter that we all need.

A. APPEARANCES

Okay, admittedly, this is the most frivolous of my suggestions, but I confess that I needed an "A" to complete my acronym ("GRACES"), so bear with me. For better or worse, our culture places considerable value on appearance. It just does. So, you have my permission to do anything that might qualify as a little "vain," short of transforming yourself into Joan Rivers or Michael Jackson. There is nothing wrong with investing some effort (and money) into looking better if it makes you *feel* better. Of course, the best approach to looking better includes good nutrition, adequate sleep, and fitness activities, but more superficial indulgences are fine up to a point. A great haircut, a new wardrobe, teeth whitening, hair restoration, a modest amount of Botox, even some minor surgery (in the right hands) are all okay, if they make you feel better.

C. CREATIVITY

I love to take photographs, especially portraits of people. Afterward, I go home and edit them, cropping the images and fixing exposure errors. When I'm engrossed in that process, I literally lose track of time. For a while at least, I forget whatever minor troubles are hassling me, and I give my brain a break from the stressors of daily life. I am willing to bet that the creative process of picture taking and editing releases some of the "feel good" hormones in my brain.

For other people, the same phenomenon occurs when they plant and tend a garden. People who paint or sculpt get lost in their work, as do writers and musicians. So, reunite your old garage band! You will be doing something creative and "reconnecting" as well. Two for one! Go ahead and annoy the neighbors. Tell them I said it was "doctor's orders!"

As adults, many of us have completely stopped *playing* in the way we did so naturally as children. Maybe we need to free ourselves to be sillier and more whimsical again, at least in short bursts.

So, absorb yourself regularly in something creative, ideally every day, even if it's only for fifteen minutes. Start playing the trombone. Or the kazoo! Build a replica of the Taj Mahal out of popsicle sticks or Legos. Put together a giant jigsaw puzzle. Explore new ideas. Exercise your imagination. It's your call.

Give yourself permission to be playful. And don't worry about how you look or sound to anyone else.

E. EXERCISE

There is a theory that all truth is contained in television sneaker commercials. When it comes to exercise, that truth is "Just do it." Ideally, for three or four days a week. Ideally, for forty-five minutes or more. Ideally, with your heart rate up so you can feel your heart and lungs working, and you break a sweat, but you could still talk to someone without gasping. If you love technology, get one of those wrist bands that add up the miles and calories. If you don't love electronic gadgets, don't bother.

If you're out of shape, start modestly and build up gradually. Any cardio exercise is fine. Resistance training with weights is also great and has been shown to preserve muscle mass and bone density as we age. Sports are wonderful, especially when they get you outside. Consider an athletic trainer, if you can afford one, to coach you and to make you feel guilty if you should happen to miss a workout. Consider a health club, especially if you live in a climate (Boston!) that is unfriendly for half the year.

If your joints bother you, go swimming. Play music through earbuds if your workouts seem boring. And if you are ever on the fence about whether or not to exercise because you are a little tired or feel pressed for time . . . *just do it*! Your brain's "feel good" chemicals will let you know that you made the right choice—every time.

S. SPIRITUALITY

Who am I to speak about spirituality? The cosmos is a mystery to me. But I do feel that I can say this: every one of us wants to feel "connected." Connected to something beyond ourselves. To something that makes us part of a larger family. To something that suggests that we belong somehow in the vast, unknowable schemes of the universe.

Many people worry that the spiritual underpinnings of our culture have been dissipating in recent years, and I agree with them. And I think our souls yearn more than ever for those deeper connections. If we can find them, we are less likely to grapple with depression and anxiety and more able to deal with tragedy and loss.

What connects us spiritually to the world around us? For the author of *A Walk in the Woods*, it is trudging along the Appalachian Trail. That wouldn't do it for me (I can't handle mosquitoes, and I like hot showers), but it apparently does for a lot of people. The attendance in houses of worship seems to be declining, but those congregations still fill the need for many.

The truth is that there are as many answers to this question as there are people. We all would like to find a connection, a source of inner peace, a spiritual dimension in our lives. Yoga, tai chi, and many other approaches to mindfulness can be very helpful.

Whatever methods we choose, it seems to me that we all need to keep seeking the connections that are comforting to us and help us to make sense of our humanity.

So, if you have a tendency to get sad or anxious, here is a kind of homework assignment, should you decide to accept it. Some of it might seem a little silly to you. Much of it you already know. There will be no formal grades at the end of the course. These GRACES are your tools. Please take them out of the toolbox and put them to use:

(G) Do something charitable. If you are already doing something charitable, do even more of it. Keep doing it.

(R) For seven days, contact three people you are losing touch with. Texts, emails, even postcards are fine, but an old-fashioned phone call might be even better. Then, keep working at reconnecting.

(A) Get some new clothes, a great haircut, or have your dermatologist laser your age spots. Looking better in the mirror is a nice thing. (Don't forget this includes fitness, eating well, and sleeping enough.)

(C) Set aside time for creativity.

(E) Exercise consistently.

(S) Explore your spirituality. Learn to meditate. Go to a house of worship. Walk in the woods. Get a telescope. Pick something that resonates with you and go with it.

If you are willing to commit to these GRACES, I am quite sure that you will feel better, even in these often-troubling times. If you don't, kindly see your health care provider or counselor for further assistance.

A Case Study:

One of my Type A patients, an expert at "multitasking," took my office handout on GRACES to heart. When I saw him the next year for a check-up, he told me that he had organized a group of his college buddies to train together for the Boston Marathon—and to raise money for research on a type of cancer that had killed one of their classmates. After their training runs, the group gathers at a coffee shop and laughs.

When I saw my patient, he was smiling. He had lost weight and looked healthy. He had cleverly figured out a way to multitask and address just about all of the GRACES in a single, sustained project.

Well done!

ADDITIONAL RESOURCES

Steven Gardner Photography: stevengardnerphotography.com
Camp Jabberwocky: campjabberwocky.org
The Ashmere Project: ashmereproject.org
Zeno Mountain Farm: zenomountainfarm.org
AccesSportAmerica: accessportamerica.org
HandReach: handreach.org
New England Holocaust Memorial: nehm.org
Children's Memorial at Edgartown Lighthouse: mvmuseum.org

ABOUT THE AUTHOR

Dr. Steven Gardner is a member of the honorary staff of the Massachusetts General Hospital (MGH) and Harvard Medical School following a lengthy career as a clinician and teacher in internal medicine. As a member of the MGH Global Disaster Response Team, he served as a chief medical officer in Haiti and the Philippines with Project Hope. For twenty-five years, he was a volunteer physician at the Martha's Vineyard Cerebral Palsy Camp (Camp Jabberwocky), caring for children and adults with a wide range of challenges. He is a passionate photographer whose images focus on the resilience of people facing adversity and the compassion of the people who assist them. Dr. Gardner is a past winner of the Harvard Medical School Humanism in Medicine Award.

His first book, the Wall Street Journal Bestseller *Jabberwocky: Lessons of Love from a Boy Who Never Spoke,* is an inspirational and loving portrait of a handicapped boy who enriched the lives of all who knew him and changed how people think about disabilities. In this new collection of short stories, Dr. Gardner examines the surprising connections among people from different walks of life, connections that reveal our common humanity and provide hope in a troubled time.